CAROLINE GARCIA

Lingam Massage Revealed

How To Give Sexual Pleasure To A Man So He Never Forgets You

Copyright ©

Preface: The Forgotten Essence of Male Pleasure

Welcome, dear reader.

I am honored to have you on the pages of this journey that, I promise, will be revealing. My name is Carolina Garcia and, although it may seem presumptuous, I am truly thrilled that you have chosen this book. Not only because it is a project into which I have poured years of experience, research and dedication, but also because I know that your choice reflects a desire for growth and understanding, a path to a deeper connection with both yourself and those with whom you share intimate moments.

The decision to embark on this journey with me is not only an act of curiosity, it is a reflection of your intuition and inner wisdom. I am convinced that every person who decides to delve into the depths of understanding and pleasure has an inner voice that guides them to self-discovery. And if you have felt that this book is the right one for you, trust that feeling.

While I have traveled many roads in my life, one of my greatest prides is being recognized as a professional in this field. But beyond the professional label, I am someone who genuinely cares about sharing knowledge in a way that can transform lives. I appreciate the vulnerability, curiosity and desire that comes with approaching topics as intimate and profound as the ones we will address.

Within these pages, you will discover the universe of male pleasure from perspectives you may never have considered. From the ancient art of Tantra and its relationship to Lingam massage, through practical techniques, to the deep emotional and spiritual bonds that can be built through this art. Each chapter has been designed to take you step-by-step, from the basics to more advanced techniques, backed by real stories and practical advice.

Perhaps, at some point, you will be tempted to put the book aside. That's natural; facing the unknown can be challenging. But I encourage you to continue, to take a deep breath and move on page after page. Because at the end of this journey, you will not only have gained skills and techniques, but also a deeper understanding of yourself and those with whom you share your intimacy. The emotional benefits of that understanding are invaluable, offering a kind of connection and satisfaction that transcends the physical.

In short, I thank you. Thank you for trusting me, my experience and this work. And most of all, thank you for trusting yourself and your ability to grow, learn and connect in deeper and more meaningful ways.

With sincerity and appreciation,

Carolina Garcia.

Chapter 1: Lingam Massage: More Than Just a Massage

Have you ever felt that intimacy is something that goes far beyond the simple physical act? In the pages of this book, we will explore the richness and depth of that idea. But, before we get into technical details and ancient techniques, let me ask you a question: Are you ready to rediscover pleasure, not only as a physical act but also as a spiritual and emotional experience?

Lingam massage, at first glance, might seem to be simply a technique to increase male pleasure. But, as you will see, it is much more than that. It is an invitation to a deeper connection with oneself and one's partner, a tool to heal, to relax and to explore the limits of one's own body and mind.

Why is it so important to know and master this technique? Well, imagine you have spent your whole life listening to a song, but you have only heard half of the notes. Lingam massage is like discovering those missing notes and allowing yourself to enjoy the full melody for the first time.

You may wonder why, with all the information available in the digital age, there is still so much ignorance or misunderstanding about male pleasure. The reason is that, despite our apparent "openness" in matters of sexuality, we are still captive to taboos and prejudices. Most people do not take the time to really understand what pleasure is, reducing it to simple orgasms or ephemeral moments.

However, as you may have already noticed in the preface, our exploration of this topic is going to go much further. **Yes**, we are going to talk about techniques and tactics. **Yes**, we will go into anatomical details. But all of that will be the framework within which we will explore a much larger and deeper idea.

For a moment, think about the times you have experienced pleasure - has it always been the same, or have you noticed nuances and variations, moments of ecstasy that are more intense than others? The key is to understand that each experience is unique and that, with the right tools, we can amplify and enhance those experiences.

So, dear reader, I promise you that this journey will be eye-opening. Not only will you learn techniques that will change your sex life, but you will also discover aspects of yourself that you may never have considered. It is a journey of self-discovery, and I guarantee it will be worth every step of the way.

With each page, I hope you feel excitement, anticipation and, most of all, gratitude for allowing yourself this opportunity for growth and understanding. And now, as we delve into the roots of Tantra and its relationship to Lingam massage, I invite you to keep an open mind and a willing heart. Because, at the end of the day, isn't that what we all seek? A genuine, authentic and deep connection, not only with our partner, but with ourselves.

So, take a deep breath, relax and get ready for the journey. Because, after all, Lingam massage is much more than just a massage, it is a journey into an unexplored universe of pleasure. Are you ready to embark on this adventure?

The journey we are undertaking takes us through centuries of wisdom and practice. We are not the first to try to understand the secrets of the human body and its capacity for pleasure. In this regard, it is often helpful to look into the past and see what our ancestors knew about the art of Lingam massage and how they integrated it into their lives.

In "The Tantric Dance of Love", *Ravi Ananda* (1995) tells us that Lingam massage was more than an act of love; it was a form of meditation, a way of connecting with the universe. If we consider this perspective, we realize that what we are doing is not simply providing or receiving physical pleasure, but that we are opening ourselves to a much greater and transcendent experience.

Joanne Kellerman in "Sensual Touch: Rediscovering Intimacy" (2007) explains how, over the centuries, techniques and practices have evolved. However, the essence remains the same: the search for a deeper connection, not only with our partner, but also with ourselves. Kellerman argues that, deep down, we all crave that connection, that feeling of being fully present and in tune with another person.

And you know what? She's right. Think about it for a moment. **How many times have you felt truly connected to someone?** How many times have you felt like you were sharing something that went beyond the physical, something that touched your soul? Those are the experiences we remember, the ones that leave a mark on us. And those are the experiences that Lingam massage can help us reach.

Geoffrey Malins in "The Path to Ecstasy: A Study in Tantric Sexuality" (2012) goes further and challenges us to reconsider our own relationship to pleasure. He argues that modern society often reduces pleasure to something that is quickly consumed and forgotten. But Lingam massage offers us something different, something that is both ancient and deeply relevant to our modern lives.

So here we are, at the crossroads of history and modernity, searching for the wisdom our ancestors knew intuitively and trying to adapt it to our world today. Isn't it exciting to think that, even in this fast-paced and often impersonal world, we can still find ways to connect in meaningful ways?

One thing all these authors agree on is the importance of **intention**. It's not simply about following a set of step-by-step instructions (although, of course, we'll get to that). It's about approaching Lingam massage (and, indeed, any act of intimacy) with an open mind and a willing heart.

Dear reader, what we are discovering together is something truly special. But, like any journey, there are challenges along the way. However, I am confident that, armed with the knowledge and wisdom of the ages, you will be more than prepared to face them. And, as we'll see in the following chapters, every challenge is also an opportunity to grow, learn and, above all, connect. Are you ready to move forward? Because what's ahead is even more exciting.

But to really understand the power of Lingam massage, let's dive deeper into its roots and concrete practices. For that, let's consider a couple of examples that perfectly illustrate its impact.

Think of *David*, a senior executive in an international corporation. He works long hours, is always on the go and rarely takes a moment for himself. On the surface, he seems to have it all: success, money, respect. But inside, there's an emptiness, a sense of disconnection. David came across Lingam massage through a workshop he decided to take out of pure curiosity. Through this practice, he not only experienced levels of pleasure he had never known, but also reconnected with parts of himself he had forgotten. He realized that, beyond the physical pleasure, was the opportunity to experience deep healing and spiritual connection.

Or consider *Linda* and *Roberto*. They were married for more than 20 years and, over time, the spark and connection they initially shared began to fade. They had fallen into a rut and, although they still loved each other, they felt something was missing. It was Linda who discovered Lingam massage through **Evelyn Stone's** "The Transcendence of Touch" (2003). Determined to reintroduce passion and connection into their relationship, she began exploring this practice with Roberto. Through their sessions together, they not only rediscovered physical pleasure, but also revived the emotional and spiritual bond that had brought them together in the first place.

These examples are not simply stories; they are testimonials to the transformative power of Lingam massage. And the exciting thing is that these are not isolated cases. All over the world, people of all backgrounds, ages and life experiences are discovering and rediscovering the power of this ancient practice.

According to **Marcia Hanson** in "The Awakening of Pleasure: Stories and Practices from the Tantric World" (2010), Lingam massage is more than a technique, it is a path to self-awareness and self-transformation. By practicing, one not only connects with one's partner, but also reconnects with one's own body and one's own essence.

What about you, have you ever felt disconnected, not only from others, but from yourself? Have you ever longed for an experience that takes you out of the monotony and transports you to a space of pure ecstasy and connection? If so, you're in the right place.

Let me ask you one more question: **are you ready to embark on this journey of self-discovery and pleasure?** Because if you are willing to dive in with an open mind and heart, the rewards are beyond what you can imagine. And, as you'll learn in the coming chapters, Lingam massage is just the beginning. There's a whole world of practices and techniques waiting to be explored, each with its own set of benefits and joys. Let's get to it!

Thus, the journey through the world of Lingam massage leads us to profound revelations about ourselves and how we relate to others. It is as if we have been walking through a garden on a dark night, with only the moon to guide us, and suddenly, the clouds disperse and thousands of stars illuminate our path, showing us the richness and depth of everything around us.

To further contextualize the magnitude of this practice, **Dr. Anil Kumar** in his work "Tantra: Energy and Essence" (1997), mentions that Tantra, of which Lingam massage is an extension, is more than just a technique; it is a philosophy of life. It is a way of seeing and experiencing the world. And through Lingam massage, this philosophy manifests itself in a physical and palpable form, giving us an opportunity to experience ecstasy and connection in its purest form.

These revelations and experiences are not the end, but only the beginning. Like a musician learning to play an instrument, at first, the notes may seem out of tune or disconnected. But with practice and dedication, soon those individual notes come together to form a harmonious and beautiful melody. Similarly, as we delve deeper into the practice of Lingam massage and explore its various techniques and nuances, we begin to see how all of these individual pieces come together to form a holistic and transformative experience.

Now, dear reader, it is your turn to take the reins. What tune do you want to play? What kind of connection and ecstasy do you want to experience in your life? The choice is yours and the tools are here, in your hands, waiting to be used.

I hope you are intrigued, stimulated, even a little challenged. And you should be. Because, as you will learn in **Chapter 2**, Tantra, from which Lingam massage is derived, has ancient roots, intertwined with stories, cultures and traditions that have been passed down from generation to generation. You will benefit from understanding the origins and connections to Lingam, and how this rich history influences the practices and techniques used today.

So, as we move forward, let me make you a promise: if you commit to this journey, if you go into it with an open mind and a willing heart, in the end, you will not only discover the art of Lingam massage, but you will also discover yourself in ways you never imagined.

The next chapter awaits you, and with it, a journey into the very heart of Tantric energy and its interconnection with Lingam massage. Prepare yourself for an odyssey that merges past, present and future in a dance of ecstasy and connection. The adventure is just beginning.

Chapter 2: The Art of Tantra: Origins and Connections with Lingam

The art of Tantra. Just hearing that term, perhaps your mind automatically transports you to an exotic place, full of mystical rituals and unbridled passion. But what is Tantra really, and how does it relate to the Lingam massage we explored in the previous chapter? Let me guide you through this exciting path that unfolds before us.

First, it is vital to understand why this theme is essential. Imagine for a moment a house: solid, sturdy and beautiful. Lingam massage would be one of the rooms in that house. But to fully understand it, you must explore its foundation. That is Tantra. It is the foundation upon which the entire edifice of conscious, connected pleasure is erected. Have you ever wondered how some of the most intimate sexual practices originated? If you have felt that curiosity, then you are in the right place.

Tantra is often thought to be solely about sexuality. And, while it is true that it involves sexual energy, to reduce it to that alone would be like saying that the ocean is simply water. Do you feel that spark of curiosity burning? That's because your mind has already begun to delve into the depths of the Tantric art.

Tantra, in essence, is an ancient tradition that encompasses much more than just sexuality. It focuses on connection, energy and union. Remember the feeling of being fully present, connected to everything and everyone around you? That is the essence of Tantra. It is a tool to achieve that connection and presence in all aspects of life, including sexual. It is full consciousness, divine connection and understanding of the universe and oneself.

As we explore more deeply in the following segments, I invite you to reflect: what is your personal perception of Tantra? Do you see it simply as a set of sexual techniques or as a philosophy of life? Now, what if I told you it could be both at the same time?

Don't get me wrong, there are no wrong answers here. However, it is crucial to begin this journey with an open mind and a willingness to learn. In this chapter, we will unravel the mysteries surrounding Tantra, tracing its history, its practices and, most importantly, its connection to Lingam massage.

To end this introduction, let me ask you one more question: are you ready to immerse yourself in a world where history, spirituality and passion intertwine in an eternal dance? If your answer is yes, take a deep breath, keep an open mind and move on. The adventure is about to begin.

Speaking of timeless dances, Tantra has been one of those dances that has evolved and adapted over the centuries. Before we dive into the depths of its connection with Lingam massage, it is essential to understand where this ancient art comes from.

When we go back to the origins of Tantra, we find ourselves in ancient India, around 500 BC. Here, this philosophy was born as a way to achieve self-realization and union with the divine. Unlike traditional religions that often separated the physical from the spiritual, Tantra taught that sexual energy, when channeled correctly, could be a path to spiritual enlightenment. Imagine for a moment a flowing river. That river, in its natural course, has the power to shape landscapes, nourish lands and sustain lives. In the same way, Tantra saw sexual energy as that powerful river, which if directed in the right way, could shape souls and nurture spiritualities.

The scholar André Padoux, in his work "Tantra: The Path of Ecstasy" (1990), highlights how Tantra was not simply a way to improve intimate relationships, but a complete path to understanding the duality of existence. Think about it: the duality of passion and peace, of desire and detachment, of self and universe. This interplay of opposites is a dance that has always been present in our lives.

Now, when we speak of Tantra in the Western context, its interpretation has undergone numerous transformations. In fact, many Westerners have become familiar with Tantra largely through the popularization of its application in intimacy and sexuality. Oskar Ratti and Adele Westbrook, in their acclaimed book "Secrets of Tantra" (1979), describe how Tantra, upon reaching the West, merged with various movements and philosophies, giving it a distinctly different flavor from the original. This, of course, is not necessarily negative. Each culture takes and adapts the teachings according to its own needs and perspectives.

However, it is essential to recognize that Tantra is not just a series of sensual techniques to enhance the intimate life, although it certainly can include that. It is a path to a deeper understanding of ourselves and the universe. When we connect this philosophy with Lingam massage, we are not simply talking about massage techniques; we are talking about the union of energies, the channeling of sexual power toward enlightenment and a deeper understanding of the self.

Do you realize how everything is interconnected? Pleasure, passion, peace, purpose... all these facets of our existence have a common thread in the art of Tantra.

As we move forward, keep that idea of interconnectedness in mind. Visualize how each learning, each technique and each philosophy intertwine, forming a beautiful and complex fabric that is, in essence, the art of living and loving fully. And as you do, remember that this is not just an ancient story, it is your story too. The story of how each of us seeks to understand, experience and express our deepest and truest energy.

In order for you to truly appreciate the depth of this connection between Tantra and Lingam massage, let me guide you through some concrete examples, for nothing clarifies an abstract concept better than a palpable account, anchored in reality.

Think, for a moment, about the essence of meditation. In the art of meditation, one focuses on the present, connects with the breath, and seeks to free the mind from distractions, right? Now, imagine transferring that same concentration and presence to an intimate encounter. Imagine feeling every sensation, every touch, every pulse as if it were a mantra running through your body. This is exactly what Tantra teaches us.

For example, in the Tantric tradition, there is a technique known as *Maithuna*, which can be roughly translated as "union". It is not simply a physical act, but a spiritual ritual.

In fact, in the seminal work "Tantra: The Tradition of Shiva and Shakti" (1985) by Rajesh Dixit, it is illustrated how, during Maithuna, couples not only seek pleasure, but strive to reach a heightened state of consciousness through their connection.

Translating this to Lingam massage, we can see how it is not simply an act of giving and receiving pleasure, but a ritual where the giver and receiver connect on a much deeper and spiritual level. It is a dance of energies, where each touch is an affirmation of respect, adoration and connection.

Another example that gives us clarity about the relationship between Tantra and Lingam is found in the technique of "connected breathing". In the book "Breathing and Tantra" (1992) by Anand Sharabi, it is explained how the breath is the key to channeling and controlling Kundalini energy, a life force that resides at the base of the spine. By learning to breathe together, giver and receiver can synchronize their energies and elevate the act of massage to a spiritual level.

You are probably thinking, "This sounds wonderful, but how do I apply it in practice?" That's an excellent question, and precisely in later chapters we will go into practical details. But for now, it's vital that you understand the theoretical and philosophical foundation behind it all. Because, after all, without understanding, any technique simply becomes empty motions.

As we move through this chapter, I want you to feel the depth and richness of this ancient art. I want you to visualize how every practice, every technique, every teaching of Tantra has a purpose and a story behind it. And in the end, you will see how all of this converges to enrich and elevate the Lingam massage experience, taking it beyond the mere physical act and transforming it into a sacred ritual of connection and spirituality.

We've come a long way in this chapter, haven't we? From the ancient origins of Tantra to the intimate connection it shares with Lingam massage. Every paragraph, every word, has been designed to bring you to a deeper understanding, to make you feel, almost tangibly, the pulse of this ancient art.

In your reflections, you may have found yourself drawing parallels between what we have discussed and your own experiences, or perhaps imagining what it would be like to incorporate these concepts into your life. The beauty of Tantra and Lingam massage lies in their universality; they are practices that transcend culture, time and space, and have the power to enrich our lives in ways we may never imagine.

It is curious how something that seems so physical, so tangible, can be, at the same time, so spiritual and ethereal. As David Frawley would say in "Tantra: The Path of Acceptance" (2003), "Tantra is the bridge between the physical and spiritual worlds, a tool to transcend the limitations of the flesh and connect with the divine that resides in each of us."

And now, as we prepare to close this chapter, I invite you to pause and reflect. Imagine yourself in a quiet sanctuary, surrounded by soft lights and intoxicating scents. In front of you, a candle flickers, and as you focus on the flame, you feel your breathing become deeper, more rhythmic. It is a safe space, a place of introspection and growth.

With this picture in mind, let me tell you something: the best is yet to come.

In the next chapter, we will delve into the intricate anatomy of male pleasure. While knowledge of Tantra and Lingam massage is fundamental, understanding the physiology behind the techniques is equally crucial. I promise it will be a fascinating journey, an eye-opening exploration of the wonders of the human body.

Are you ready to discover the male universe from a whole new perspective? Ready to unravel the mysteries that have eluded many for so long? Then take a deep breath, and join me. Because, trust me, you won't want to miss what's coming next.

Chapter 3: Anatomy of Pleasure: Discovering the Male Universe

In the vast universe of human pleasure, there is one territory that remains largely unexplored and shrouded in mystery: the male anatomy of pleasure. Why, you may ask, in an age where information seems to be at the click of a button, does it remain such an enigmatic terrain? Perhaps because, throughout history, male sexuality has largely been viewed as a one-dimensional phenomenon. But you and I, dear reader, know that it is much more than that.

Imagine for a moment a musical instrument that has been played the same way for years. Although it produces pleasant sounds, its true potential has never been explored. Now, imagine that you decide to learn more about that instrument. You begin to play different strings, vary the rhythm and experiment with different techniques. Suddenly, you discover sounds and melodies you never knew existed. This is the promise of this chapter: to discover the symphony of pleasures hidden in the male body.

Now, have you ever looked at a detailed map? On it, every road, river, and mountain has a purpose and tells a story. Similarly, every part of the male anatomy has a function, a purpose, and more importantly, an often overlooked capacity for pleasure. Are you ready to unfold that map and embark on this journey of discovery?

By immersing yourself in the male anatomy of pleasure, you are embarking on an adventure into a deeper understanding of what it means to be a man in the most intimate and profound sense. Not only will you learn about biology, but you will also explore how culture, history and society have shaped perceptions and experiences of male pleasure.

We have previously mentioned the art of Tantra and Lingam massage, and how these ancient practices celebrate energy and pleasure (see Chapter 2: The Art of Tantra: Origins and Connections to Lingam). These practices show us that, since time immemorial, cultures have understood the complexity of male pleasure. However, modern science and erotic literature also have much to offer in our exploration.

Let me quote Dr. Alan P. Brauer, author of "Eros and Miracles: The Secrets of Male Sexual Potency" (1991), who noted that "understanding the male sexual anatomy is the first step toward a full and enriching erotic experience". Brauer shows us that, beyond the penis, there is an orchestra of erogenous zones waiting to be discovered and celebrated.

Take, for example, the frenulum. This small, often overlooked band of tissue is incredibly sensitive and can offer waves of pleasure when stimulated correctly. Or consider the perineum, that area between the testicles and the anus, which is a highway of nerves and sensations. Did you know that proper stimulation of this area can enhance and prolong male pleasure? And that's just the tip of the iceberg.

Now, the famous author and sexologist John Money, in his work "Love and Amorology" (1980), tells us: "The male body, in its totality, is a temple of sensations and erogenous potentials". Money invites us to consider that every inch of skin, every whisper of hair, has the potential to be a source of pleasure.

So why is this rich tapestry of pleasure still so undervalued? It could be because of cultural norms that dictate that men should always be "strong" and "in control," relegating the exploration of their own anatomy and pleasure to the back burner. But here, dear reader, we challenge you to break those molds and embark on a journey towards discovering your own body.

Imagine for a moment that you are in a museum. Each gallery and exhibit offers you a new perspective, a new way of seeing the world. In the same way, every part of your anatomy is a gallery of sensations waiting to be explored. Isn't it exciting to think of all the wonders waiting to be discovered?

But, before I continue, I'd like to propose a question, for you to ponder for a moment: when was the last time you really took the time to explore and appreciate every nook and cranny of your anatomy without haste, without expectation, just for the sheer pleasure of discovery? If you can't remember or never have, this chapter is your gateway to that journey.

Let's talk now about concrete examples, those that put into perspective the richness of the male anatomy. A man, let's call him Javier, once confessed to me an experience that changed his perspective on self-pleasure. While taking a hot bath, he decided, on impulse, to slowly explore every part of his body, from the scalp to the soles of his feet. At first, he felt a little uncomfortable, almost as if he was doing something he shouldn't be. But as he continued, he began to discover spots on his body that he had never considered erogenous zones. The crease behind her knees, the curve of her hip, even her earlobe. Each discovery was like a revelation, a little spark of pleasure that showed her that her body was a treasure trove of sensations.

Now, leaving aside this individual testimony, let us consider what Margot Anand says in "The Art of Tantric Ecstasy" (1995). Anand talks about the 'Wheel of Passion', a tantric map of the human body, which identifies various points of energy and pleasure. It is fascinating how ancient traditions, separated by millennia and thousands of miles, came to the same conclusion: the male body is replete with pleasure points, beyond the genitals.

Imagine that your body is an unknown landscape, full of mountains, valleys and hidden rivers. Wouldn't you like to be the pioneer explorer of that terrain? Aren't you intrigued by what you might find?

Another author, Beverly Engel, in "Male Passion: Unleashing the Power of Desire" (2000), presents us with an interesting analogy. She compares the male body to a musical instrument, where each string, each key, responds to a different melody, a unique frequency of pleasure. The key, Engel says, is to learn to play that instrument with skill and sensitivity, rather than simply striking it in the hope of getting a response.

Laugh if you want, but there is truth in that comparison. And you don't need to be a master musician to learn to play this "instrument". All you need is patience, curiosity and, most importantly, the desire to discover yourself in a way you may never have considered before.

At this point, you are likely to feel a mixture of excitement, curiosity and, perhaps, a touch of nervousness. It's completely natural. We're challenging cultural and social norms that have been ingrained for centuries. But isn't it exciting to be a rebel in the name of one's own pleasure? Let's delve deeper into this universe and discover together what awaits.

As we move forward in this exploration, we cannot fail to mention the research of Alfred Kinsey, who in "Sexual Behavior in the Human Male" (1948) revolutionized the way we understand male sexuality. Kinsey, through thousands of interviews, determined that men's capacity for pleasure is vast and varied, far beyond what the society of the time believed.

And this is where the big question leads us: how many possibilities have we set aside simply because we don't dare to explore? The limitations we impose on ourselves, driven by prejudice and fear, have led us to experience only a fraction of the pleasure we were meant to experience.

Take for example the delicate skin between the testicles and the anus, the perineum. Often overlooked, this region is rich in nerve endings and can be an incredible source of pleasure when properly stimulated. Or consider the frenulum, that elastic band of tissue that connects the head of the penis to the shaft; for many, it is an incredibly sensitive area that can generate surges of pleasure.

But, as Thomas Moore said in "The Soul of Sex" (1998), "Sex is about the soul as much as it is about the body." Beyond the physical points and erogenous zones, there is the emotional and spiritual connection that is created by understanding, accepting and celebrating our bodies in all their glory.

And you know what? That's just the tip of the iceberg. We've covered a lot of ground in this chapter, but there's still so much more to discover and experience. The beauty of this journey is that it is infinitely customizable. Each person will find their own path, their own pleasure zones, and their own moments of revelation.

Now if you're excited about what you've learned so far, wait for what's coming in the next chapter. Essential preparations for the ritual? Yes, I'll talk about tools, oils and how to use them to enhance the Lingam massage experience. Your intimate life is about to be elevated to a whole new level, where every encounter will be a dance of sensations and emotions. Are you ready to dive even deeper into this journey of self-discovery? Because, dear reader, this is just the beginning. Go ahead, take that step into the next chapter. Ecstasy awaits you.

Chapter 4: Tools and Oils: Essential Preparations for the Ritual

Have you ever attended a classical music concert and marveled at the virtuosity of the musician? You can appreciate every note, every vibration and the passion with which he plays the piece. Now, imagine if that musician, instead of a beautiful Stradivarius violin, had a simple toy guitar. Would the result be the same? Clearly not. The tool, in this case the instrument, plays a crucial role in the mastery of the final result.

Now, why are we talking about music in a book dedicated to Lingam massage? For a very simple reason: just like in music, in massage, tools and preparations are essential to reach the desired ecstasy. And of course, we are not only talking about the hands, although they are our main tool, but everything that can elevate the experience.

Lingam massage is not just a set of techniques, it is a ritual. And like any ritual, it requires preparation. Throughout this chapter, I will introduce you to the fascinating world of essential oils and tools that will allow you to create a transcendental experience.

The first question that might arise is, is it really so important what kind of oil or tool we use? Isn't the right intention and techniques enough? Ah, dear reader, that would be like trying to paint the Sistine Chapel with crayons. Yes, the art resides in the artist, but the right tools allow that art to reach its full splendor.

Think of oil not just as a lubricant, but as a conductor of energy, a medium that will allow you to glide your hands smoothly and fluidly, creating indescribable sensations. Now, you may be wondering, "How do I choose the right oil?" And this is where we get into interesting territory.

Different oils have different properties. For example, coconut oil, celebrated by authors such as Sarah Balzac in "The Mystique of Natural Oils" (2003), not only offers a perfect glide, but also has antibacterial properties and nourishes the skin. Or almond oil, mentioned by David Tomlinson in "The Alchemy of Touch" (2010) as an ideal medium for sensual massages, thanks to its light texture and moisturizing capacity.

And here's a little humorous touch for you: imagine trying to do a massage with olive oil? You'd come out smelling like salad!

But beyond oil, there are other tools that can intensify the experience. Have you considered using feathers, silks or even crystals? Each of these elements has the potential to awaken different sensations, taking massage to a whole new level.

I hope you are already feeling the curiosity and excitement to explore all of these options. As we move forward, I will guide you in the choice and proper use of these tools, making sure you are prepared to deliver an unforgettable Lingam experience.

Now, take a deep breath and dive into this chapter, where the possibilities are as vast as your imagination and your desire to bring pleasure. Because in the end, dear reader, Lingam massage is a gift, a dance, a connection... and it deserves to be celebrated with the best possible preparation. Are you ready to discover it? Of course you are.

So, as we dive deeper into this ocean of knowledge, we can perceive the importance of the right choice. Just as a chef selects the freshest ingredients for his signature dish, the Lingam massage practitioner must be equally meticulous in the selection of his oils and tools. Have you ever stopped to consider the vast world of possibilities behind a single drop of essential oil?

Look, ylang-ylang essential oil, for example, has been cited numerous times for its aphrodisiac properties. Patricia Evans in her book "Essential Oils for Sensual Bliss" (1998), details how this particular oil can enhance libido and reduce stress and anxiety, thus creating a more conducive environment for intimacy. So, imagine combining ylang-ylang with a carrier oil such as almond oil to maximize its effectiveness in massage?

On the other hand, have you heard of rosehip oil? Not only is it known for its incredible moisturizing ability, but as Lorraine Sanders mentions in "The Sensual Art of Touch" (2007), it also has the ability to balance energies and promote a deeper connection between giver and receiver.

In addition to oils, the choice of the right tools can vary the texture and rhythm of the massage. A feather, for example, can be used to gently caress, causing chills and awakening the skin. Hot stones, on the other hand, can bring warmth and depth to certain areas of the body, increasing blood flow and the feeling of relaxation.

Richard Hargreaves' "Tools of Sensual Awakening" (2012) discusses how different cultures have incorporated various tools into their sensual rituals. From the soft silks of Asia to the hides and skins of Native American traditions, there are endless possibilities waiting to be explored. So, dear reader, why limit yourself to the hands when the world offers such a vast repertoire?

Certainly, you may think it's overwhelming with so many options to consider. But isn't it exciting? After all, every choice you make, every combination of oils and tools, will be an extension of your personality and your intentions. It's a dance of aromas, textures and sensations that you can offer your partner, creating unforgettable moments and unique experiences.

But there is something I want you to remember: while oils and tools are essential, they are just that, tools. The real magic lies in your intentions, in your connection, in your ability to read and respond to your partner's needs and desires. So, as you immerse yourself in the world of oils and tools, don't forget to also immerse yourself and your partner, because that's where the true art of Lingam massage lies.

Like sailing on an enchanted sea, the selection of oils and tools is not the only part of this journey; there are specific techniques for application that can turn an already sensual experience into something transcendental. In your mind's eye, picture a blank canvas; do you realize that the choice of brush and painting technique will determine the final work? Likewise, the technique you use when applying the oils and tools will influence the final result of the Lingam massage.

As an example, let me tell you about the "light feather" technique. With this technique, extremely delicate movements are used, almost like the brushing of a feather on the skin. The intention is not to exert pressure, but simply to awaken the skin. In her work "The Sensations of Touch" (2015), Emily Crawford details how gentle, almost imperceptible movements can heighten the level of arousal and anticipation, making each subsequent touch even more intense.

Now, what happens if we combine that technique with the ylang-ylang oil we mentioned earlier? The recipient of the massage can experience a flurry of sensations, from the intoxicating aroma to the smooth glide of the oil, enhanced by the almost ethereal brush of the light feather. You can imagine the skin bristling, every nerve ending awakening and craving more.

On the other hand, consider the "rhythmic pressure" technique, which, as the name implies, employs constant, rhythmic pressure on specific points. It is not a painful pressure, but rather one that relieves tension and releases blockages. Geoffrey Thompson, in "Deep Sensations: Unlocking Hidden Pleasures" (2009), illustrates how appropriate pressure at key points can trigger a release of pent-up energies, leading the recipient to deep states of relaxation and pleasure.

That said, don't you find it fascinating how the combination of oil, tool and technique can orchestrate a symphony of sensations? It's like a dance in which every step, every turn, every movement, is perfectly coordinated to bring the dancing partner (in this case, the giver and the receiver) into a state of ecstasy and harmony.

Of course, practice makes perfect. Knowledge of these techniques and their proper application will require time, experimentation and, above all, communication with your partner. But remember, the journey itself is as pleasurable as the destination. And each time you practice, you will discover something new, something surprising, something that will bring you even closer to mastering the art of Lingam massage.

We have traveled together through a sea of possibilities, gliding through the rich texture of the oils, feeling the delicate dance of the techniques, and discovering the tools that will allow us to take Lingam massage to the next level. Do you feel that curiosity sweeping over you? That is the sign that you are on the right path, the path to mastery.

However, you may be asking yourself, "So after selecting the right oil and knowing the techniques, what's next?" This is where a crucial aspect comes into play: atmosphere. Imagine for a moment that you're in an orchestra and each musician is tuning his or her instrument. You can have the best violinist in the world, but if the atmosphere isn't right, if the sound of conversations, creaking chairs or noise from outside interferes, the magic is lost.

The same goes for Lingam massage. You could be the most skilled in the techniques, but if the setting isn't right, the experience will be dulled. This is how Anthony Wren describes it in "Ambient Pleasures: The Importance of Setting" (2017), where he highlights how atmosphere plays a key role in any connection ritual.

Now, if you feel your heart pounding with longing to discover how to create that perfect space, that sanctuary of pleasure and connection, I have good news. The next chapter, dear reader, is about just that. We'll discover together how light, sound, scent and the arrangement of space can be powerful allies in your journey to ecstasy. And not only that, you'll learn how small details can completely transform the experience.

Are you ready to dive into that dimension where every element conspires to bring you and your partner into a state of complete harmony? If you feel that tingle of anticipation, that thrill that runs through you from head to toe, I invite you to continue. Open the door to the next chapter and let yourself be enveloped in the art of creating the perfect ambiance. Because, at the end of the day, the stage is as much the protagonist as the actors on it.

Chapter 5: The Importance of Atmosphere: Creating the Perfect Space

Have you ever walked into a room and, for no apparent reason, felt a surge of calm and peace? Or perhaps, you have entered a place and immediately felt restless or anxious. Space, dear reader, has incredible power. Some would say it is magical. And in the context of Lingam massage, this power comes alive in ways you might not imagine.

Now, you might be thinking, "Why should I care so much about atmosphere if what really matters is technique?" Well, here comes a question for you: have you ever tried to relax amidst the deafening noise of a bustling city or find concentration in a cluttered room? It's not easy, is it?

The atmosphere, dear reader, is not simply a background or a stage. It is an active participant in the ritual. It is the canvas on which the experience is painted, the foundation upon which the ritual is built. It is, in many ways, the first step in ensuring that Lingam massage is an unforgettable experience.

So, if we accept that atmosphere is essential, the natural question is: how do we create it? Ah, and this is where things get interesting. Because, just as in cooking, where a pinch of salt can transform a dish, in atmosphere, the smallest details can have a profound impact.

Before we go any deeper, I invite you to close your eyes for a moment. Imagine you are in a place where you feel completely safe, loved and accepted. A place where every sound, scent and sensation combines to wrap you in a warm and comforting embrace. How does it feel? What do you see, hear, smell? Keep that image in your mind as we continue.

You're beginning to understand, aren't you? Atmosphere is not a simple addition, it is an intrinsic part of the experience. And if you really want your partner to never forget you, if you really want to take Lingam massage to the next level, then it is essential that you understand and master the art of creating the perfect atmosphere.

Let's put the Lingam massage aside for a moment. Think about your most memorable moments. Maybe it was a romantic dinner at a restaurant, where everything from the music to the lighting created an atmosphere you simply couldn't forget. Or maybe it was that getaway to a luxury spa, where every detail, no matter how small, was meticulously cared for to ensure your relaxation and well-being.

See what I'm getting at? In both examples, the experience wasn't simply about the food or the massage. It was about how those elements combined in a specific environment to create something transcendent.

And therein lies the power of atmosphere. It is the difference between the ordinary and the extraordinary. Between the forgettable and the unforgettable.

In the following segments, we'll delve more deeply into exactly how you can create this atmosphere and what elements you should consider. Because, just like any artist, you have a palette of options at your disposal. And with the right tools and a little knowledge, you can paint a masterpiece.

Are you ready to embark on this exciting journey and discover the secrets of the perfect atmosphere? I promise it will be a journey that will forever change the way you see and experience Lingam massage. So take a deep breath, open your mind and heart, and let's go forward together on this fascinating journey.

After this powerful recognition of the importance of atmosphere, one might ask, "So what are the keys to creating that perfect space, that ambiance that envelops and immerses the receiver in an ocean of pleasurable sensations?" Well, look no further than the sages of old, those who understood deeply the mysteries of the senses and how to use them to elevate any experience to something sacred.

Sarah Fielding, in her work "The Art of Sensuality" (1978), pointed out that "Sensation is not simply feeling, but how you feel it." This statement seems obvious, but is often overlooked. It's not just what you put in the space, but how you put it, how you coordinate it, and how you make it interact with the other elements.

Let's start with something that is often overlooked: lighting. Light has the unique ability to change the perception of a space. Think of the difference between a candlelit room and one with bright fluorescent lighting. One invites intimacy, mystery, exploration; the other is functional but lacks warmth and character. Consider investing in scented candles, or dimmable lights. A subtle trick, mentioned by Mark Havers in "Architecture of the Soul" (2003), is to use mirrors strategically to reflect candlelight, multiplying its effect and creating a mystical effect.

Then there is scent. Smell is one of our most powerful senses and can evoke memories and emotions with a simple inhalation. Whether you choose incense, essential oils or diffusers, the scent should be consistent with the experience you are trying to create. Lavender, for example, is known for its relaxing properties, while jasmine can increase arousal and sensuality. You know that scent that instantly takes you back to a particular place or time? Therein lies its power.

Sound is another crucial component. Music, or even the sounds of nature, can be the bridge that takes the recipient from the everyday to a realm of pleasure. It's not just about choosing a random playlist, but finding those rhythms, those melodies that resonate with what you're trying to convey. Daniel Ketterman in "The Power of Sound" (1995) points out how certain frequencies can help align and balance the chakras, facilitating a deeper, more connected experience.

Last but not least, there's texture. From the sheets you choose to the towels, every tactile element contributes to the experience. Something as simple as an Egyptian cotton sheet instead of a regular sheet can change the feel of the entire ritual.

In conclusion, creating the perfect atmosphere is an orchestra of details, where each plays its part, but together they create a symphony of sensations. And yes, while the Lingam massage technique is essential, without the right atmosphere, it is like a beautiful musical instrument played in an empty room.

So, are you ready to dive even deeper into this art and discover how each of these elements can be tuned to perfection? Because, dear reader, we are about to enter an even deeper journey, one that will not only enlighten your mind but also your soul.

Imagine for a moment a corner of your home that has always seemed special to you, but you never knew exactly how to take advantage of it. Do you have it in mind? Now, visualize that corner becoming a sanctuary of pleasure and relaxation, a space where the outside world disappears and only sensations remain.

Every detail counts, and as we have already learned, it is crucial to consider each element individually and as part of a whole. But how do we translate all this into concrete actions? Let's look at some practical examples.

The perfect corner

Take for example a terrace that has been underutilized for years. You could start by installing light curtains that move with the wind, not only to provide privacy but to create a play of light and shadow as the sun moves. Jacqueline Heartworth in "Spaces of Intimacy" (1989) points out how half-open areas can have a special charm, allowing the sounds of nature, such as birdsong or the murmur of the wind, to integrate into the environment.

The   aromatic   touch
Let's say you decide to do a massage at sunset. You could make use of a diffuser with rose essential oil. Not only for its intoxicating aroma, but because, as Peter Holms points out in "The Complete Guide to Aromatherapy" (2001), roses have properties that relax the mind and uplift the spirit.

The   Power   of   Water

If you're lucky enough to have a small pond or fountain, the sound of water can be hypnotically relaxing. But even if you don't, why not consider a small device that simulates the sound of flowing water? Marianne Thompson, in her work "Natural Elements in Intimate Spaces" (2015), points out how water can act as a bridge between our inner self and the outer world, reminding us of the constant flow of energy and life.

The   choice   of   textiles

We already mentioned the importance of textures, but let's look at a more concrete example. Suppose you have chosen an interior room for your ritual. You might opt for soft, plush cushions on the floor, surrounded by wool or silk blankets. According to Gregor Stein in "Textures and Sensations" (1997), the choice of textiles can make the difference between feeling in an ordinary place or in a personalized sanctuary.

These examples show us how, with a little creativity and attention to detail, any space can be transformed. And as you begin this journey of creation, you'll notice how this process not only enhances the Lingam massage experience, but also connects you more deeply with your own senses and desires.

And now, as this chapter begins to draw to a close, it is time to consolidate all that we have learned and prepare for the surprises that the next chapter has in store for us. Because, at the end of the day, every step in this journey is designed to lead you to a deeper understanding and a richer experience. Because, after all, pleasure is an art, and you are on your way to becoming a true master.

Sit for a moment and take a deep breath in. Feel the air travel through your lungs, fill your chest and then escape on an exhale. In this simple act of breathing, you have connected with a daily ritual that most of us take for granted. However, if you manage to notice the nuances in the simplest acts, then you are ready to dive deeper into the art of pleasure.

We have journeyed together through the process of transforming a space into a sanctuary. It's not simply about cushions and scents, it's about the intention behind each choice. It's about creating a space where both the giver and the receiver can feel safe and connected. As Patricia O'Sullivan noted in "The Dance of Space" (2003), "The space we inhabit is an extension of ourselves; it reflects us, nurtures us, and sustains us."

Every element, whether it's a candle, a fabric, or the very air you breathe, is loaded with possibilities. David L. Hanson in "The Alchemy of Spaces" (2010) writes, "Every corner of a space is like a blank page, waiting for the ink of our intentions and desires." So, when you spend time choosing a fabric, selecting a scent or adjusting the lighting, you are writing a story of pleasure, connection and revelation.

Now, you may be asking yourself: "And after you have created this perfect space, what next?" Ah, dear reader, therein lies the real magic! Because creating the perfect atmosphere is just the beginning. Once you have the stage, it's time to embark on the journey.

And it is precisely that journey that we will talk about in the next chapter. How breath and energy can open doors to deeper connection and unexplored pleasure. How can simple breathing take us beyond what we have known? What are the techniques that can enhance the Lingam massage experience? All this and more awaits you.

So, are you ready to dive into the depths of your being, to discover hidden secrets and to connect with your essence in a way you never imagined? I invite you to go ahead, to let yourself go and to embrace each new discovery with curiosity and wonder.

The next chapter is an invitation, an open door to a new dimension of pleasure and knowledge. And I promise you that once you walk through that door, your perspective on pleasure, intimacy and connection will be forever changed. Because, after all, we are on a journey of revelation, and each step is a promise of something greater to come. Do you dare to take the next step?

Chapter 6: Breath and Energy: The Key to Deep Connection

Allow me, dear reader, to ask you a simple question: How many times a day do you stop to truly be aware of your breathing? To feel, really feel, how the air enters and leaves your lungs? Perhaps the answer will surprise you. In a world where speed and immediacy are the norm, stopping to observe something as essential and basic as our breathing seems like a luxury, doesn't it?

Now, have you ever wondered why breathing is so crucial in ancient practices such as yoga, meditation, and yes, Tantra? The answer is simple but profound: the breath is the gateway to our vital energy, the link between body and mind. It is, in essence, the key to deep connection.

When thinking of Tantra and Lingam massage, many imagine manual techniques, postures and movements. However, without correct breathing, all these acts are just that: acts. Empty. Lacking the power they promise. You'd be surprised how much breathing can influence pleasure and connection.

The importance of breathing is not a new concept. In fact, several authors throughout history have emphasized its role in our daily lives. As Annette Wilson pointed out in her book "The Breath of Life" (1997), "Breath is not only the act of keeping us alive, it is the compass that guides us to our deepest essence".

Have you ever felt that electricity coursing through your body during a moment of intense pleasure? That current that connects you with something greater, that makes you forget everything else, taking you to an almost transcendental state. That, dear reader, is energy in its purest state. And I assure you, the path to reach that state begins with the breath.

If I told you that you could enhance your connection with your partner, intensify pleasure and access higher states of consciousness simply by learning to breathe correctly, would you try it? Imagine for a moment that each inhalation and exhalation has the power to bring you closer to a deep connection, not only with your partner, but with yourself.

Don't get me wrong, the road is not easy. It takes practice, patience and, above all, intention. But isn't it worth it? After all, if you're reading this book, it's because you're looking for more. More pleasure, more connection, more understanding. And I promise you, at the end of this journey, you'll find exactly what you're looking for and so much more.

So, will you join me in this exploration? Together we will discover the art of breathing and how it can be the key to a deeper connection. Throughout this chapter, I will offer you the tools and knowledge you need to get started. Are you ready to breathe deeply and dive into the depths of Tantra?

The act of breathing is both voluntary and involuntary, a perfect conjunction between the conscious and the subconscious. It accompanies us in every moment, even when we are not aware of it. In the context of Tantra, breathing takes on a leading role, and no wonder. It becomes the vehicle that transports the energy, that energy that we seek to channel during the Lingam massage.

You have heard of the kundalini energy, right? Rooted at the base of the spine, this energetic serpent, as it is often called, lies dormant, waiting to be awakened. When awakened and rising through the chakras, it can bring experiences of heightened awareness, deep pleasure and unparalleled connection. But how is it awakened? Well, this is where the breath comes in.

Not surprisingly, renowned authors in the world of Tantra have emphasized breathing. Richard Landon, in his work "The Awakening of the Serpent" (2005), argues that "Conscious breathing is the bridge between the physical body and subtle energy. It is the catalyst that awakens and channels the kundalini".

Now, well, it's not simply a matter of breathing deeper or faster. There is art and science to it. Tantric breathing goes beyond getting oxygen into our lungs; it is about an energetic exchange, about feeling how each inhalation and exhalation moves energy, connecting us more intimately with ourselves and with our partner.

You might ask: How can something so simple be so transformative? And you're not alone in this concern. When Samantha Hughes published "Breathe, Connect, Love" (2012), many people were skeptical. However, she argues, "Simplicity is deceptive. Something as basic as breathing, when done with intention and awareness, can trigger inner revolutions."

And this is where Lingam massage comes in. Imagine you are applying the techniques learned in the previous chapters. As your hands move, your breath synchronizes with your partner's, creating a rhythm, a flow. The energy intensifies, moves, and soon, what began as a simple massage becomes a dance of intertwined energies.

Remember, if at any time you feel lost or overwhelmed, you can go back to Chapter 5, where we discussed the importance of creating the right atmosphere. The right atmosphere and a mind focused on the breath are the foundation for a successful Lingam massage.

Don't be afraid to immerse yourself in this practice. Allow yourself to experience, feel and connect. The rewards, as you will discover, are immense. And, if you feel you need more guidance, don't worry, we will continue to explore more on this fascinating topic. For now, keep breathing, keep feeling.

The journey through the path of Tantra and the deep connection we establish with our breath is subtle and revealing. It makes us realize the magnitude of our own existence, and the resonance our being has with the universe. I invite you to dive even deeper into the art of Tantric breathing and explore how this bridge between the physical and spiritual world can enhance the Lingam massage experience.

But how can we achieve this elevation of energy, this harmonious singing between two beings?

Example 1: Imagine you are in a forest. The air is fresh and every time you inhale, you feel the energy of nature fill your body. Now, bring that same feeling into an intimate room. When you are with your partner, close your eyes and imagine that you are inhaling that same pure energy and exhaling any tension or worry. This simple yet powerful visualization connects you to the here and now, and creates an open channel for the flow of energy between you and your partner.

Harold Jensen, in "The Echo of Breath" (1998), argues that "By allowing our breath to be our guide, we open a portal to a realm of deeper connection and understanding." That is, beyond a simple physical act, the breath takes us on a journey through dimensions of consciousness, opening doors to sensations and experiences previously unknown.

Example 2: Think of an accordion. As it expands, it sucks in air, and as it compresses, it expels air, creating music. Our lungs work in a similar way, but instead of music, we create life. Now, when combined with the Lingam massage technique, that "music" can become a symphony of pleasure and connection.

Now, have you ever stopped to think about the power of breath combined with intention? In the context of Lingam massage, intention is key. It is not just touching, it is communicating, it is transmitting, it is feeling.

As Mary Lou Richardson proposes in her work "Breathing with Purpose" (2010), "By combining the breath with clear intention, it is as if we light a beacon in the darkness, illuminating our path and allowing us to move forward with certainty and purpose."

This is crucial in Lingam massage. Every touch, every caress, must be guided by breath and intention. In this way, you are not only providing pleasure, you are opening a channel of deep communication with your partner, establishing a connection that transcends the physical.

However, breathing is not an isolated tool. In the next segment, I will show you how to combine these breathing techniques with the power of conscious touch, taking the Lingam massage experience to new heights. For now, breathe, feel, and allow yourself to be the conductor of this symphony of sensations.

As we delve deeper into the art of conscious breathing and its role in Lingam massage, we inevitably come to an understanding: energy flows where intention goes. Just as a river follows its natural course, sexual and spiritual energy follows the path laid out by our intention and our breath. By mastering these elements, we can create truly transformative experiences.

We cannot fail to mention Lucia Browne, who in "The Dance of Breath" (2005), mentions, "Life itself is a dance of inhalations and exhalations, a delicate balance between giving and receiving. When we tune into this natural rhythm, our experiences become richer, more vibrant." It is a constant reminder that something as simple as breathing, can be the key to previously unknown worlds of pleasure and connection.

You may be asking yourself, how does all this integrate into the actual practice of Lingam massage? The answer, my dear reader, is through synergy. The harmonious combination of breath, intention and touch.

Example: Imagine a candle burning in a dark room. The simple act of lighting it changes the whole atmosphere. The light illuminates, the warmth radiates. Now, imagine that candle is your intention, the room is your massage space, and the air that keeps the flame burning is your breath. Each component is essential to keeping that flame bright and warm. If one fails, the experience changes. The key is to keep everything in balance.

Before concluding this chapter, a humorous pause: Why are yogis so good at Lingam massage? Because they really know how to "inhale the moment". But jokes aside! How seriously we approach this practice determines the level of benefit and satisfaction we can gain and offer.

Now, I sense that you have been waiting impatiently, but with a deeper understanding of breath and energy. And here you are, on the brink of even greater knowledge, ready to dive into the waters of conscious touch. Are you ready to discover the magic of touch, the sensitivity that is often overlooked in masculinity, and how this understanding can open doors to even deeper connection?

In the next chapter, "The Power of Conscious Touch: Recognizing Male Sensitivity," we will dive into the world of touch, the connective tissue that binds all the components of Lingam massage together. If you thought you already knew what touch is, get ready to rediscover it and look at it in a whole new light.

So, are you ready to move on? Because the path of discovery and pleasure is just a breath away. Let's move forward together. I promise you, it will be an unforgettable journey.

Chapter 7: The power of conscious touch: Recognizing Masculine Sensitivity

Human beings have always had a strong desire to connect, and it is in the power of touch where we find the most genuine and vulnerable manifestation of this desire. Now, have you ever stopped to think about the power of a simple touch, how, sometimes, with a single caress you can feel that you can read another person's soul?

Touch, dear reader, is a language in itself, a language we all speak, but which few master. In the realm of male intimacy, this mastery takes on a new dimension. Yes, masculinity has been, for too long, a bastion of strength and resistance, and perhaps, for that reason, we have forgotten that beneath that shell there is a sea of sensitivity waiting to be explored and honored.

The delicacy of conscious touch is a revelation. It transforms a simple massage into a sensory experience, a dance of energies flowing between two beings. But why is it so essential to recognize male sensitivity in this context?

The power of conscious touch lies in its ability to connect us to the here and now. It is in this present that the magic happens. And when we connect with that level of sensitivity in man, we are acknowledging an essential part of his being that is often obscured by societal expectations and stereotypes. Lingam Massage, as we discussed in the previous chapters, is a ritual that celebrates this sensitivity.

But what happens when we recognize this dimension? In the words of Arthur Matthews in "The Awakening of Touch" (1997), "By recognizing the sensitivity in the other, we are, in fact, recognizing their humanity. And in doing so, we connect more deeply with our own." Now, imagine the magnitude of this discovery in the context of intimacy. It's revolutionary!

Let me ask you a question: how many times have you touched or been touched in an authentic way, where each touch conveyed a message, a feeling, an intention? If your answer is rarely or never, don't worry. You are about to embark on a journey of rediscovery and connection. Because, at the end of the day, what is life if not a series of connections and shared experiences?

This chapter invites you to dive into the science and art of conscious touch. Through it, you will not only learn to touch, but also to feel, to connect and, most importantly, to communicate without words. After all, in the game of pleasure, hands are not just tools; they are instruments of love, attention and recognition.

Are you up for discovering more? Because, if so, the road ahead is fascinating, and I guarantee it will change the way you see and experience intimacy. And as we move forward, I promise you one thing: laughter, revelations and, yes, lots of "Aha!".

But what if I told you there was more to this journey? Not just the how, but also the why. Experts, scientists and masters of Tantra have spent years researching and developing techniques that enhance the power of conscious touch, and their wisdom will be our guide. Because, as I mentioned earlier, this is an art and, like any art, it requires study, practice and passion. So take a deep breath, relax and get ready to dive into an ocean of sensations. The adventure has just begun.

As I mentioned, the art of conscious touch has been the subject of study for millennia. But what happens when we take that touch into the sphere of intimacy? It becomes a language. A wordless dialogue where the hands express what the soul feels. Now, this art, although innate, has been refined and perfected over the years.

In her work "The Secret Language of Touch" (2002), Helena Rowley argues that every human being has a unique map of sensations. Imagine, for a moment, that the skin is a canvas. Each caress, a brush stroke that awakens a different color, a different emotion. And in the context of masculinity, this canvas is often full of undiscovered colors, waiting to be revealed.

So how do we discover this map? We start with an open mind and willing hands to explore. But herein lies the challenge: in our modern society, so hurried, so disconnected, we have forgotten how to touch and be touched in an authentic way. Have you ever stopped to think about the last time you really felt a caress? Not a superficial caress, but one that penetrates the layers of your being, that reaches to the very core of your soul.

Benjamin Stewart, in "The Ways of the Skin" (1998), gives us a revealing insight: "Touch is not only a mechanical function, but also a gateway to emotional and spiritual connection." It is a truth that, although it seems obvious, we often forget.

Every touch has the capacity to be a bridge, a connection, a dialogue.

And it is in this dialogue that the true power of conscious touch is found. It is not just a technique or a method; it is a philosophy, a way of living and connecting. It is seeing the other, feeling the other and, in the process, finding oneself.

Have you ever wondered why certain touches make you shudder while others go unnoticed? It's because, beyond the physical touch, there is intention, energy and connection. And in the context of Lingam Massage, this is magnified exponentially.

I challenge you to pause and remember a moment where a caress took your breath away, where you felt like time stood still and all that existed was you and that feeling. Got it? Good. Now, imagine being able to create that moment, not just for yourself, but for your partner as well. That's the promise of conscious touch.

As we move forward in this chapter, I invite you to keep that image, that feeling, as your compass. Because, at the end of the day, beyond techniques, methods and theories, what we are really looking for is connection. An authentic, deep and transformative connection. And I promise you, dear reader, it's a journey worth taking.

And so, dear reader, I lead you through this fascinating labyrinth of sensations and connections. But as every good navigator knows, it's not just about knowing the destination, it's about understanding the journey. And in the art of conscious touch, every step, every caress, every sigh is an essential part of that journey. Join me as we dive into examples that will illuminate your path.

Imagine you are on a quiet beach, the sun is about to set and the sea breeze caresses your skin. You feel its freshness, but also the residual heat of the departing day. That duality, that contrast is similar to the art of conscious touch. It is the ability to evoke and balance different sensations, to give and receive, to explore and let yourself be explored.

Anna Lafayette in "The Embrace of the Wind" (2005) relates an experience where a simple touch, executed with full awareness and attention, was more powerful than years of superficial interaction. She recounts how, in a tantric massage session, a therapist used a feather to trace imaginary lines on her back. That seemingly simple act awakened memories, emotions and connections in her that had been dormant for years.

Why? Because this therapist understood something fundamental: conscious touch is not about force, but about intention. It is the art of listening with the hands, responding to signals, however faint, and taking the person on an inner journey of discovery.

Now, bringing this into the context of masculinity and Lingam Massage is even more momentous. Traditionally, male sensitivity has been relegated to the background, hidden behind masks of strength and resilience. But what if I told you that behind that shell is an ocean of sensations waiting to be discovered?

Think about it. Imagine that every inch of skin is an unknown continent, full of mountains, valleys and secrets. If you trace a path through that landscape with full attention, you will discover routes and treasures you never imagined. It is a journey that not only redefines pleasure, but also connection and mutual understanding.

Take, for example, the inside of the wrist. It may seem like an innocuous place, but as Albert G. Johannson mentions in "The Cartography of Pleasure" (1995), it is an area rich in nerve endings, a gateway to the nervous system. If you apply light pressure and trace slow circles in that area, you might evoke deep, relaxing sensations, a reminder that conscious touch goes beyond the obvious places.

But what if we take this further, if we explore areas that have traditionally been seen as taboo or simply overlooked? This is where the magic happens, where the deepest connections are forged. And yes, we'll talk more about this in subsequent chapters, but for now, I invite you to keep an open mind and a willing heart.

This is the power of conscious touch: the ability to discover, to connect, to transform. It is a dance between giver and receiver, a conversation without words. And you, dear reader, hold the key to unlock this world. So, are you ready to move forward? Because I promise you, the journey is just beginning.

That sense of wonder, of standing on the edge of an abyss full of unexplored possibilities, is what defines the true essence of conscious touch. And as you travel this path, each step takes you deeper, closer to that core of pure understanding and authentic connection. It is a place where silence speaks louder than any words, and where every whisper of skin has the power to transform.

Within this silent dance, there are secrets waiting to be unveiled, stories yearning to be told. Richard Fallow in "The Ocean Beneath the Skin" (2002) writes about the infinite capacity of the human body to feel, to connect, to love. According to him, the skin is the canvas on which our stories are written, and every touch, every caress, is a brushstroke in that unfinished painting.

However, like any masterpiece, it requires patience, practice and, above all, passion. It is the passion to discover, to understand, to connect. And if there is one lesson you should take with you, it is that conscious touch is not simply a technique, it is an art. An art that transcends the physical to touch the soul.

Now, you might ask, "If it's so powerful, why didn't I know about it? Why is it such a well-guarded treasure?" The answer is simple: because in our quest for immediate gratification, we often forget the power of pause, of silence, of slow, methodical exploration.

Have you ever stopped to think about how many nuances you can feel with a simple touch? Or how many stories can be told through the rhythm of a heartbeat? It's a vast and deep world, and you are about to immerse yourself in it.

And what to expect from the next chapter? Oh, dear reader, you are in for a journey that will take you from the most basic fundamentals to the most exquisite and refined techniques. A place where the art of massage intertwines with ancient wisdom to create an unparalleled experience. You will delve into techniques that will not only evoke pleasure, but will open doors to dimensions of connection that you may not have known existed.

And yes, you may feel resistance, skepticism, maybe even fear. But I promise you, with every page you turn, with every technique you explore, you will come one step closer to that core of pure connection, to that space where pleasure and soul meet.

So, with a sigh of anticipation and a promise of discovery, I invite you to follow along. Because what comes next has the potential to change not only the way you view pleasure, but the way you connect with the world. Are you ready to take the next step? Because I promise you, this is a journey you won't want to miss.

Chapter 8: The Basic Techniques: Fundamentals to Get Started

Lingam massage, that term that has generated curiosity and mystery for centuries. But why is this millenary technique, designed for male pleasure, still so enigmatic in an era where information flows more freely than ever?

Before diving into the vast ocean of techniques, postures and rituals that Lingam massage encompasses, it is essential to have a firm understanding of the foundation upon which this ancient practice is built. Imagine trying to build a skyscraper without a solid foundation; it would sway at the slightest breath of wind. Similarly, Lingam massage needs a solid foundation for its benefits to be profound and lasting.

Now, have you ever stopped to think about what makes a touch, a simple touch, can trigger a wave of sensations, emotions and even internal transformations? Is it just a matter of technique or is there something deeper and more spiritual at play? Reflect for a moment... When you touch with intention, with knowledge, and, above all, with love and connection, doesn't that become a sacred act?

The importance of learning the basic techniques lies not only in knowing where and how to play. It is also about understanding the philosophy behind each movement, each breath, each pause. Remember, every touch is a conversation, and as in any dialogue, it is not only about talking, but also about listening.

But why is it vital to start with basic techniques? Well, as Michael Breus used to say in *The Power of Sleep* (2016), "Before you run, you must first learn to walk." These techniques are the first steps on your journey into the art of Lingam massage. They are the tools that will allow you to transcend from the mundane to the mystical, from simple touch to sublime connection.

And, to add a little humor, have you ever tried to assemble a piece of furniture without reading the instructions? If you did, you probably had pieces left over or they didn't fit right, right? Similarly, Lingam massage, while an art, also has a science to it. And for everything to "fit," it's essential to know and practice the basic techniques.

In the previous chapters, we have already explored the rich history of Tantra and how it connects to Lingam, the anatomy of male pleasure and the importance of creating the right environment. All of this lays the groundwork for what comes next. However, if you feel the need for a refresher on any of these concepts, I invite you to return to the previous chapters (Chapter 1 through 7) to strengthen your understanding.

So, dear reader, are you ready to embark on this odyssey of discovery? Because, once you master these basic techniques, I promise that your journey to ecstasy and spiritual connection will be more fluid and transcendental. And the exciting thing is that this is just the beginning of a journey into a deeper understanding of self and other.

Now, as we dive into the basic techniques, it is vital to consider some words of wisdom from noted sex therapist David Schnarch in his work *Perpetual Passion* (1997). He said,

"Sex is not something we do, but an expression of who we are." So, Lingam massage goes beyond simple movements; it is about genuinely expressing who we are, connecting with our essence and that of the receiver.

The first technique we will explore is **mindfulness**. Yes, it may sound strange for us to consider it a 'technique', but it is fundamental. Before your hands touch the body, your mind must touch the present moment. Like a moving meditation, feel every inch of skin, observe the reactions, listen to the breath, and connect with the emotions that flow. Let your mind be completely absorbed by the experience, like when you immerse yourself in a good book and forget everything else around you.

Another basic technique is the **rhythm of synchronized breathing**. In *The Breath of Life* (2004), Sarah Elliot mentions that the breath is the key that unlocks our emotional and physical barriers. By synchronizing your breath with the receiver's, you are not only harmonizing your energies, but also building a bridge of connection and understanding. It is like dancing in unison, moving together in perfect harmony.

The hands, those magical instruments we all possess. **Light touch** is the next technique to master. It is not about pressing hard, but touching gently enough to awaken every nerve, every skin fiber. The skin, after all, is the largest organ in the body and is full of sensitive receptors. By touching in this way, you are sending waves of pleasure coursing through the entire body. Imagine the caress of a feather or the gentle brush of the wind, and so should be your movements.

Remember the popular saying "practice makes perfect"? Well, in the world of Lingam massage, this adage takes on even greater importance. Conscious practice is essential. Not just practice for the sake of it, but with intention, with a desire to improve, to connect and to bring pleasure.

A smile can light up a room, and in this context, it can also light up the soul. Do not underestimate the power of humor and laughter in this process. In the middle of a session, a genuine smile, a light laugh can relieve tensions and build an atmosphere of confidence and joy.

These basic techniques, although they may seem simple at first glance, have the potential to radically change the Lingam massage experience. If at any time you feel overwhelmed or confused, you can always go back to Chapter 6: Breath and Energy, to remind yourself of the importance of connection through the breath.

Dear reader, I hope you feel inspired and excited about what is coming next. The doors of knowledge and experience are open, waiting for you to cross the threshold into a world of pleasure, connection and understanding. The key is in your hands, or rather, in your hands and in your heart. And if you wonder what else there is to discover, I promise you that the depths of this practice are as vast as the ocean, and we are about to dive even deeper.

Now, we will delve into the art of **varied pressure**. In *Touch: The Forgotten Sense* (2012), Laurence Fenton describes how different degrees of pressure can arouse different sensations and emotions. Imagine a light rain caressing your skin, compared to the invigorating impact of a waterfall. In Lingam massage, varying the pressure is like playing the keys of a piano, creating a symphony of sensations that can range from the most delicate whisper to the most passionate crescendo.

Let me give you a concrete example. Imagine you are touching the base of the Lingam. Start with a gentle, barely perceptible touch, as if you were brushing the petal of a rose. Then gradually increase that pressure, feeling the response of the tissue under your fingers, observing the receiver's reaction, listening to his nonverbal signals. Does he feel a shudder of pleasure or a slight contraction? Your ability to read these responses and adjust your touch is essential.

Another fascinating technique is **the "spiraling" technique**. Here, the movement is circular, and like water running down a drain, your hands move in concentric spirals. This technique can be especially pleasurable when applied at the base of the Lingam or around the perineum. But don't just take my word for it. Margaret Daniels, in her book *Circles of Passion* (1998), highlights how circular movements can simulate waves of pleasure moving through the body.

And, as always, practice makes perfect. Remember the first time you tried to ride a bike? You probably fell off more than once. But over time, your body learned balance and rhythm. Likewise, at first, these techniques may seem strange or difficult, but with practice and patience, they will become second nature to you.

Let me tell you a little anecdote to illustrate this point. A student of mine, Carlos, was always getting frustrated because he felt he didn't "get" the techniques. During one session, I jokingly told him to imagine that the Lingam was like melted ice cream and his hands were two eager children trying to pick up every drop. The laughter we shared was unforgettable! And, surprisingly enough, that humorous image helped him relax and connect in a more authentic and playful way.

Of course, each individual is unique, and what works for one may not be right for another. That's why it's essential to keep communication open and responsive, adjusting your techniques according to the responses you observe and feel. And if you ever feel lost, feel free to return to Chapter 7, where we discuss the power of conscious touch.

So far, we have explored various techniques and I have provided you with examples to help you visualize and practice in your mind. However, the journey is far from over. As you move forward on this path of discovery and connection, you will realize that each experience is an opportunity to learn, grow and deepen in the art of Lingam massage.

Chapter 9: Massaging the Lingam: The Path to Ecstasy

Have you ever felt that tension in the air before a storm? That precise moment where everything seems to be in suspense, waiting for something wonderful, transformative. That's the feeling many people describe when they venture into Lingam massage. It is an art as old as time itself, and throughout this chapter, I will guide you down that path that has led so many to unimaginable ecstasy.

Now, why is this particular technique so important? Imagine for a moment that you hold in your hands an ancient musical instrument. One that has been passed down through the generations, with melodies and harmonies waiting to be discovered by the right player. The Lingam, in many traditions, is considered just that: a divine instrument, a portal to mystical experiences and deep states of pleasure.

And what happens when you learn to play that instrument expertly? You awaken symphonies of sensations, waves of pleasure that sweep through body, mind and soul. But here comes a crucial question, dear reader: Are you willing to embark on this journey of discovery and perfection?

In *The Dance of Pleasure* (2005), acclaimed author and sexuality expert Lucien Delacroix mentions that "the Lingam, more than an anatomical part, is a sanctuary of energy and life. Through it, we can access hidden dimensions of the human being, and, as masseurs, become the guardians of this sacred portal".

You may wonder, if this method is so powerful and transformative, why is it not more widely known or practiced? The answer lies in our own history and how, for centuries, we have oscillated between acceptance and repression of our sexuality. And, although the techniques and teachings related to Lingam massage have been around for millennia, many have been kept secret or passed down to only a few initiates.

Yet here you are now, standing on the edge of a precipice of knowledge and experience. Every word you read, every technique you explore, will bring you closer to that hidden world, ready to be revealed.

Lingam massage is not just a physical technique; it is a journey. A journey of connection, of understanding, of realizing the immense capacity we all have to give and receive pleasure. Some would say it is a form of meditation, a practice that connects you deeply with your essence and the essence of your partner.

And, as in any journey, it is essential to have a good map and a reliable guide. That's why, in the next sections of this chapter, we will break down step by step the art of massaging the Lingam. From the simplest gestures to the most advanced techniques, all with a single purpose: to allow you to experience and share ecstasy in its purest form.

I promise you that this journey will be worth it. But before I continue, I would like to leave you with a thought: Are you willing to fully embrace this path of discovery and let yourself be carried away by its mysteries? If your answer is yes, then welcome to the path to ecstasy. And if you still have doubts, I invite you to read on, because what follows could change your life forever.

Entering into the Lingam massage technique is not simply learning mechanical movements. As with any musical instrument, it requires a perfect synchronization between the performer and the instrument, a deep connection that transcends the physical.

You may have heard the phrase, "energy flows where intention goes". And so it is. Our energy is channeled through our intentions and, at the same time, is driven by them. If we consider the Lingam as a conductor of life energy, we can begin to understand the magnitude of what we are dealing with.

Now, if there is one thing that experts in the field agree on, it is that a deep and conscious understanding of the Lingam can lead to mystical experiences. In *The Book of Awakening* (1999), Penelope D'Arco expounds a fascinating theory: "The Lingam, rather than being a simple part of the male body, is a microcosm of the entire universe. Each nerve, each vein, represents a path or pathway that, when traveled with awareness and love, can connect the one who experiences it with the stars themselves."

You may ask, how is it possible to achieve such a connection? The answer lies in the understanding that pleasure is not only physical, but energetic and spiritual. When we connect with that energy during the massage, we enter into resonance with the frequency of the universe, allowing us to access higher states of consciousness.

Imagine for a moment a guitar string. If you pluck it gently, it will emit a delicate sound. But if you apply more pressure, the tone will change. So it is with the Lingam. Each touch, each pressure, each caress emits a different "note", and when we learn to "play" masterfully, we can create symphonies of pleasure.

Have you ever stopped to think about how miraculous the human body is? The complexity, the precision, the balance. In particular, the Lingam is a masterpiece of nature, designed to receive and give pleasure. While it is true that in our modern society, we are often disconnected from this ancient wisdom, you now have the opportunity to rediscover this lost art.

Returning to our musical analogy, I invite you to consider the possibilities. If the Lingam is an instrument, how many types of music can you create with it? What melodies are waiting to be discovered? And if I told you that, as with any instrument, with the right practice and understanding, you can reach unimaginable levels of mastery, would you be willing to embark on that journey?

Don't get me wrong, the path of Lingam massage is not always easy. It requires dedication, patience and, above all, love. But the rewards are priceless. And remember, if at any time you feel lost or overwhelmed, you can always refer to Chapter 8, which explores the basic techniques to get you started on this path.

Feel free, dear reader, to take a moment to reflect on all that you have learned so far. And when you are ready, take a deep breath and continue with me on this journey to ecstasy. For, as Tantric master Ananda Marga once said in his work *The*

Path of Ecstasy (1987), "Pleasure is only the beginning, the real journey is in the soul." And that journey, dear reader, is about to become even deeper and more revealing.

Now, speaking of techniques and tactics, we will explore some that, while they may seem simple, are powerfully effective. After all, it is in the details that true mastery lies.

Imagine a landscape. A forest with trees stretching as far as the eye can see. In the distance, a river meanders gently, its waters glistening in the sun's rays. This landscape, though vast and full of wonders, also hides secrets in its finer details: the rustle of leaves, the song of a bird, the scent of fresh moss. Similarly, the art of Lingam massage is composed of both broad gestures and delicate caresses.

One of the most illustrative examples of this can be taken from Lila Rosenthal's *The Passion Chronicles* (2004). She describes a technique called "The Dawn Stroke." In her words, "It is a slow glide, almost like the first ray of sunlight across the sky at dawn. It starts at the base of the Lingam, ascending with a steady but gentle pressure, as if you were painting with a brush. The sensation for the receiver is that of a gradual awakening, a surge of energy that intensifies as the movement progresses."

Lila presents us with a vivid image with this technique. She not only tells us what to do, but invites us to feel, to imagine, to live that experience through her words. By practicing "The Dawn Stroke", you will realize how something so subtle can have a profound impact.

Now, what if I told you that there is a point on the Lingam that, when touched in the right way, can trigger waves of pleasure so intense that they resemble euphoria? It is called "The Diamond Point." To quote Rosenthal again, "This point, located slightly below the middle of the Lingam, is a jewel waiting to be discovered. By pressing it in a rhythmic, circular motion, it is possible to release deep tensions and unblock stagnant energies."

Are you intrigued? It's only natural. As you delve deeper into this art, you'll discover that there are countless secrets waiting to be unlocked. But, it's essential to remember that each person is unique. What works wonderfully for one, may not be as effective for another. Therefore, communication and attunement with your partner are crucial. As discussed in Chapter 7, the power of conscious touch is fundamental to this practice.

Have you ever heard of "star shower"? No, I'm not referring to the astronomical phenomenon, but to a massage technique. Imagine the sensation of thousands of raindrops falling on your skin, each one bringing with it a flash of pleasure. To achieve this, the fingertips are used, tapping gently and quickly over the entire length of the Lingam, like rain falling from the sky.

In the end, dear reader, it is all about exploration and discovery. There are no limits to this journey, only horizons that expand as you go along. With each technique you learn, you equip yourself with another tool in your repertoire to take your partner to previously unimaginable heights of pleasure. To speak of the art of Lingam massage is to speak of a dance of energy and sensation, of connection and empathy. It is, in its essence, a journey of two souls intertwined in a gentle and harmonious rhythm, in which the giver and receiver become one. But what if I told you that there is more? That beyond the techniques and points of arousal we have explored so far, there are hidden dimensions and unexplored territories.

Renowned sexologist Marvin Green, in his seminal work *Ecstasy Discovered* (1998), tells us, "Pleasure is like a river, constantly flowing and changing. But, like a river, it has hidden depths, undercurrents that only the true explorer can discover." And so it is, dear reader. Although we have navigated the surface waters and plunged into its depths, there is still more to discover.

Have you ever experienced a moment of connection so deep that the outside world seems to fade away? It is as if all noise, all distractions, are silenced, leaving only the music of two hearts beating in unison. That, dear reader, is the magic of true tantra. It is the power of authentic connection. But achieving it requires more than techniques; it requires authentic presence and attunement.

So far, we have drawn a map, but as any good explorer knows, a map is not the territory. It is a guide, a tool. True discovery comes from direct experience, from immersing oneself in the journey with heart and soul.

It is essential to understand that each experience is unique. What may be a direct path to ecstasy for some may require patience, exploration and adaptation for others. As we mentioned in Chapter 6, breath and energy play a crucial role in this process. They are the bridge that connects us to our inner self and our partner, and through them, we can reach previously unimaginable heights of pleasure and connection.

Of course, there is more to discover. And like a fine wine, the art of Lingam massage improves and deepens with time and practice. So, even if you already feel well-equipped with the tools and techniques we've shared, I invite you to keep going, to dive even deeper into this journey.

In the next chapter, we will address "The Forgotten Zones: Secret Hot Spots". Did you know that there are areas of the male body that are often overlooked, but when stimulated, can unleash surges of pleasure as intense as Lingam's own? Get ready for a journey of discovery, where every nook and curve is a treasure waiting to be discovered.

You are about to embark on an exploration that will take you to the true essence of male pleasure. One that goes beyond the physical and into the realm of soul and spirit. So, are you ready to discover these secrets? Because I promise, once you do, you'll never look at the art of Lingam massage the same way.

Chapter 10: The Forgotten Zones: Secret Hot Spots

In the complex and enigmatic labyrinth of male pleasure, there are unexplored territories, places that ordinary mortals often overlook. I invite you to pause for a moment. Have you ever considered that full satisfaction might reside in those little forgotten areas of the male body? Or have you simply considered that there is only one epicenter of pleasure in the male?

The answer to these questions will surprise you. Not only because it will redefine what you know about male pleasure, but because it will give you a powerful tool to deepen intimacy. Are you ready for this journey? And, more to the point, are you ready to change your preconceptions and open yourself to a world of possibilities?

The art of Lingam massage is not only focused on the male organ. At its core, it is about celebrating the whole body, about recognizing and honoring every inch of skin as a sacred temple. Now, think of all those forgotten areas we've neglected for years. Areas that cry out for attention and, when touched in the right way, can open doors to unsuspected levels of pleasure. But why is it so important to know these secret hot spots?

First and foremost, pleasure is a right. A right that we all deserve to experience to the fullest. And, by neglecting these neglected areas, we are depriving ourselves of a complete experience. Moreover, pleasure is a way to strengthen connection, to consolidate intimacy. By incorporating these zones into your massage sessions, you not only expand your repertoire of sensations, but you demonstrate a deep understanding of your partner's body and soul.

Imagine a world where the deepest secrets of the male body are no longer secrets, where every caress feels like a poem and every whisper translates into waves of pleasure. Would you like to be the master who awakens those sensations? The expert navigator who knows every corner of that vast ocean of delight?

By the end of this chapter, I guarantee you will have a deeper and more complete understanding of the forgotten zones and, with it, an unparalleled ability to take your partner on an unforgettable journey of pleasure. Isn't that what we are all looking for?

But, don't be hasty. As Jacques Antoine said, in his work "The Geography of Pleasure" (2007), "The road to discovery is not to rush towards the destination, but to savor every step, every stone and every breath of air". So, let me guide you step by step, caress by caress, towards that discovery. Together, we will explore those secret spots, learn to recognize them, touch them and celebrate them.

So, are you ready to change your perception of male pleasure forever? Because I promise you, once you start this journey, there's no turning back. And, if you ever feel like you're lost or need to be reminded of concepts previously addressed, you can always go back to Chapter 3, where we explored the "Anatomy of Pleasure."

But for now, close your eyes and visualize that map of the male body. And get ready, because we're going to add some new destinations to it, some secrets that, once revealed, will change everything you thought you knew about the art of Lingam massage.

In the annals of the history of pleasure, there are voices that have attempted to unravel the mysteries of the human body. Sarah L. Richardson in her book "Shadow Zones" (2012) comments that "the body is not just a structure of bones and muscles, but a map that unfolds before our eyes, full of secrets waiting to be discovered." And, indeed, the male body is no exception.

If we stop to think about all the times we have touched or been touched, we realize that, more often than not, we limit ourselves to conventional areas, to what society has established as "normal". But what if I told you that there are areas of the male body that, when stimulated in the right way, can generate waves of pleasure as intense as those of the Lingam? Areas that, although often forgotten, are real hidden treasures. Do you dare to discover them?

The Perineum: Located between the scrotum and the anus, this small area is incredibly sensitive. By applying gentle, steady pressure, combined with circular motions, you can send electric shocks of pleasure throughout the body. It is an area that requires delicacy and care, but when touched properly, it can be a gateway to ecstasy.

The Nipples: Often overlooked in men, the nipples are highly sensitive and receptive to caresses. They can be gently pinched, caressed or even licked. Experimenting with different types of stimulation here can trigger surprisingly pleasurable responses.

The Nape: The nape of the neck, with its soft, thin skin, is an area that responds beautifully to light caresses and gentle kisses. Just running your fingertips over this area can send shivers throughout your body.

While these areas may seem obvious to some, you'd be surprised how many people overlook their potential. And while it's true that each person is a universe and what works for one may not work for another, it's worth exploring and experimenting.

Eduardo Fernandez, in his work "The Unknown Pleasure" (1998), writes: "The skin is the largest canvas of our body, and every centimeter has a story to tell, a secret to share". And she is right. When we take the time to explore every nook and cranny, to listen to every whisper of the skin, we discover not only the secrets of the body, but also the secrets of the soul.

So, as you continue on this journey of exploration, I encourage you to dive deep, to allow yourself to discover and rediscover, to open yourself to the possibility that there is more to the male body than you ever imagined. Because, at the end of the day, the art of Lingam massage is not just about technique, it's about connection, understanding and celebrating the body as a whole.

And remember, if you ever feel you need a refresher on the importance of conscious touch, you can always go back to Chapter 7. For, after all, touch is the universal language of love and pleasure.

However, the exploration does not end there. The beauty of the human body lies in its complexity and multiplicity. As you venture beyond the more familiar zones, you will discover areas that, while less popular, have the potential to provide immense pleasure when properly stimulated.

Let's go into some of these areas together, through real and tangible examples, and perhaps, as you read, you can almost feel the sensations described.

The Neck and Ears: Think of Daniel, a 29-year-old who, upon receiving a Lingam massage, found that the gentle rubbing behind his ears and the light caress on his neck sent shivers of pleasure down his spine. The earlobes, when kissed or lightly nibbled, can intensify pleasure and increase anticipation.

The Inner Thighs: Claudia, an expert masseuse, shared how her client, Peter, used to jump in surprise when she caressed his inner thighs. This often overlooked area is incredibly sensitive and can act as an exciting prelude to the Lingam massage.

The Feet: Did you know that in the feet there are numerous reflex points directly connected to other parts of the body? Martina, in her book "Reflexology and Pleasure" (2005), describes how the stimulation of certain points on the feet can provoke sensations in completely different areas of the body. A gentle massage, especially on the arch of the foot, can be a wonderful way to relax and excite at the same time.

Now here comes a crucial point: communication. Not all men will react in the same way to stimulation of these forgotten zones. Remember when we mentioned in Chapter 3 about the

"Anatomy of Pleasure"? Yes, each body is a universe unto itself. And while the techniques are universal, the responses can be unique.

Have you ever considered how many secrets a body hides? How many stories, memories and experiences reside in every inch of skin? As a masseuse, or partner, you are in a privileged position to unravel some of these secrets, to discover areas that not even the recipient themselves knew were capable of providing so much pleasure.

Take, for example, the story of Andrew, a man who, after many years of sexual exploration, discovered a new erogenous zone while receiving a Lingam massage. During the massage, the masseuse gently caressed the area just above his pelvis, a small space of skin that is rarely touched. Andrew described a feeling of electricity spreading from that spot to the rest of his body, a sensation he had never experienced before.

Professor Jeremy Franc, in his work "The Hidden Geography of the Male Body" (1998), emphasizes that many of these "forgotten" zones are not traditionally viewed as erogenous simply because they have not been given the opportunity to be explored with the kind of intention and attention they deserve.

So what can we deduce from all this? That exploration should never cease. Every massage is an opportunity to discover, learn and connect in a deeper way. Do you feel inspired to venture beyond the known? To map pleasure on your partner's or client's skin?

Now, pause. Close your eyes for a moment and take a deep breath. Imagine that you are touching or being touched in these "forgotten" areas. How does it feel? What is your reaction? Don't underestimate the power of your imagination to guide you to a more enriching experience.

With a conscious approach and an open mind, you can take Lingam massage to unimaginable heights, beyond traditional techniques and movements. Because, after all, the art of pleasure is infinite, and there is always more to discover.

As we prepare to dive into the next section, I encourage you to retain this sense of curiosity and anticipation. There are more gems to be discovered in the next chapter. Are you ready to continue this journey of discovery and ecstasy? Because what's to come promises to be even more exciting and revealing.

Chapter 11: The snake dance: Hand coordination and rhythm

Have you ever seen a snake in motion? If you haven't, perhaps you should. There is an elegance in its dance, a rhythmic grace in the way it glides effortlessly. Its movement seems to be in harmony with the music of the universe. Now, imagine that movement applied to your hands, that smooth, flowing, rhythmic touch. Are you wondering how all this relates to Lingam massage? Well, let's get down to business!

The "snake dance," as exotic as it sounds, refers to the ability to coordinate hands and rhythm in the art of Lingam massage. Why is this so crucial? Well, think about any pleasurable experience in your life. Wasn't it the rhythm, the cadence, that really defined the intensity of the pleasure?

While it is true that we have talked about the techniques, the tools, and even the forgotten zones (remember our journey in Chapter 10), rhythm is the glue that binds everything together and takes the experience to a whole new level. It is that rhythm that awakens, intensifies, and then leads to calming sexual energy.

But make no mistake, we are not just talking about a monotonous and constant rhythm. No, true mastery lies in the ability to vary, to adapt and, above all, to *tune in to* the energy of the receiver.

Imagine for a moment that you are in a concert hall, and the pianist instead of varying his rhythms and playing with passion, simply hits one key repeatedly. No matter how much you love that note, eventually, it will begin to tire you. Monotony can kill pleasure, even in the most intimate circumstances.

So let's talk about the "why" behind the snake dance. Why, when immersing ourselves in this ocean of pleasure, is it so vital to understand rhythm? The answer is simple and, at the same time, incredibly complex. Excitement and pleasure are journeys, not destinations. If you already knew this, let me remind you, and if it's new to you, take a moment to reflect on it. In fact, when was the last time you really thought about the journey of pleasure instead of focusing solely on the destination?

The great masters of tantra, since time immemorial, have always emphasized the importance of the "how". In Clara Montfort's "Rhythms of Desire" (2004), she describes how different cultures around the world have understood and practiced this art of rhythmic variation to amplify pleasure.

Rhythm, in essence, creates a kind of trance, a hypnosis if you will. It is that state in which the receiver is lost in the sea of sensations and loses track of time and space. Sounds mystical, doesn't it? Well, it is.

So, as you consider the snake dance in Lingam massage, think of yourself as a master of rhythm, as a conductor guiding every note, every pause, and every crescendo. It's not just the touch, but how, when, and with what intensity that touch is applied.

Before I continue, I leave you with a question to ponder: How can you incorporate the art of rhythm into your own experiences, whether as giver or receiver? How can the snake dance influence your connection to pleasure?

As William Masters said in "The Dawn of Pleasure" (1979), "True skill lies not in knowing the destination, but in understanding and loving the journey." As you prepare to move deeper into the snake dance, I encourage you to embrace this journey, to immerse yourself in it and, most importantly, to let go. Because, at the end of the day, the pleasure is as much about the journey as it is about the destination.

The essence of the "snake dance" is not merely a physical technique; it is, above all, an understanding. An understanding of the subtle waves of energy that flow through our being, and how these waves can be navigated and orchestrated through the hands. However, if you are looking for a deeper understanding, immersing ourselves in the writings of experts on the subject can give us an enlightening perspective.

Anna-Lise Marten, in her influential work "Hands that Sing" (1998), addresses the role of hands in the expression of desire and love. Marten posits that our hands, beyond being mere physical tools, are extensions of our essence, our soul. By focusing attention on movement and touch, Marten argues that we can communicate and feel on levels that transcend the verbal. This concept is fundamental when considering snake dance. It is not just about how you play, but *what you* are communicating when you play.

Now, when talking about rhythm and coordination, an analogy may be useful. Think of a pianist. A pianist doesn't just play the keys; he feels the music, he lives it. Every note, every pause, has a purpose, an intention. Likewise, when practicing Lingam massage, every touch, every movement has an intention behind it. It is a silent but powerful conversation between the giver and the receiver.

Returning to the concept of rhythm, let us consider an excerpt from "The Rhythm of the Skin" (2001) by Dr. Samuel Korn. Korn highlights how different rhythms can evoke different emotional and physical responses. A slow, steady rhythm can induce a sense of calm and relaxation, while a fast, changing rhythm can raise the level of arousal. It is a game, a tug-of-war between calm and excitement, which the practitioner handles masterfully.

These concepts are not unique to Lingam massage. In fact, if you look around, you will find rhythms in everything around you. From the beat of your heart, to the cycle of your breath, to the seasons of the year. Rhythm is everywhere, and it is deeply intertwined with the human experience.

For those seeking to perfect the art of snake dancing, one suggestion would be to begin by tuning into your own natural rhythms. Breathe deeply, feel your pulse. Then, when practicing with a partner, try to tune into their rhythm, their energy. As the saying goes, "it takes two to tango". And in this intimate dance, attunement is essential.

Have you noticed how at certain times, when you are truly connected with someone, you can feel their energy, almost as if their emotions are transmitted to you without words? That is the magic of rhythmic attunement, and it is that level of connection that we aspire to achieve with the snake dance.

Remember what we learned in Chapter 6 about breath and energy. Do you see how everything intertwines? Just as in a symphony, each component plays its part in creating a harmonious and intoxicating experience.

For now, I invite you to reflect on the rhythms in your life and how they impact your mood and well-being. And, as you go through this reading, keep in mind that, in the art of Lingam massage, as in life, it's not just about getting to a destination, but enjoying the journey.
Continuing our rhythmic journey, we reach the point where we not only recognize and understand rhythm, but experience it through palpable examples.

On one occasion, during a workshop in Bali that addressed the art of tantric massage, I had the opportunity to witness a powerful demonstration. Two experts in the technique stood in the center of the room, and through the simple action of their hands in coordination, they created a dance that evoked the undulations of a majestic snake. Their movements were not hurried, but rather a series of slow, deliberate caresses that sped up and slowed down in perfect sync with the recipient's breathing.

The observation reminded me of Lillian Vermeer's "The Embrace of Silence" (2003). In it, Vermeer describes in detail the connection between giver and receiver, and how the synergy between the two can reach almost transcendent levels. "When two beings are in tune, their energies converge in a dance that defies logic and verges on the divine," she writes.

This concept of rhythmic connection is not new. In fact, it is rooted in ancient traditions from around the world. Consider, for example, African tribal dances. In these dances, the tribe gathers and moves their bodies to the beat of drums. It is not just a matter of physical movement, but a spiritual communion. Each person in the tribe feels the energy of the other and moves accordingly. It is a hypnotic and powerful spectacle, where the collective acts as a single entity.

What about mating rituals in the animal world? Watch birds of paradise in their courtship. It is a game of rhythms and precise movements that seek to enchant the partner. In this act, it is not only dexterity that is vital, but the ability to tune in to the other, to read their signals and adapt to them.

These examples from nature and culture demonstrate that rhythm and coordination are not mere abstract concepts, but tangible realities that we can observe and learn. I encourage you, as you read, to visualize these examples and reflect on how you might incorporate them into your Lingam massage practice. You will not only be improving your technique, but also deepening your connection with your partner.

Of course, the snake dance is not just about the giver. The receiver also has a pivotal role in this dance. As we mentioned in Chapter 7, the power of conscious touch is reciprocal. While the giver guides the dance, it is the receiver who, through his or her response, shapes and defines it.

In the next segment, we will explore more about how these energies converge, and how, through the serpent dance, we can reach a state of ecstasy that transcends mere physicality and enters the realm of spirit.

You can feel it, can't you? The rhythmic pulsation in the air, the whisper of energy flowing between giver and receiver. It is a synergy that is not only found in the technique, but also in the soul. Now, as you dive deeper into this world, you will discover that the art of Lingam massage is an infinitely rich and varied dance. Each movement, each caress, has its place and its purpose.

Julien Deschamps, in his revolutionary work "The Rhythm of Love" (1999), wrote: "Inside each of us, there is a melody waiting to be discovered. Sometimes it is a soft ballad, sometimes an intense symphony. The key is to tune in, to listen and, above all, to let go." That's right, letting the natural rhythm of our bodies and souls guide the dance. The snake dance is not only a technique, it is an invitation to discover the innate rhythm that we all carry within us.

This rhythm is not limited to Lingam massage. It is a universal truth that applies to all areas of our life. When we move in harmony with our inner rhythm, everything flows more easily. Decisions are made with clarity, relationships flourish and life feels more enriching.

Now, I challenge you to reflect: how many times have you really felt this rhythm in your life? At what times have you allowed it to guide you? And most importantly, how can you incorporate it more into your daily life and your Lingam massage practice?

As you immerse yourself in these reflections, I encourage you to also consider how rhythm influences emotional connection, a topic we will address in depth in the next chapter. Emotional connection goes beyond simple physical contact; it is the bridge between two souls. Imagine being able to look into your partner's eyes and feel that, without words, you are sharing a moment of mutual understanding, of deep connection. This is the promise of the next chapter. I invite you to continue this journey, to discover how looks, words and other bonds can transform a physical experience into a spiritual union.

Before closing this chapter, I leave you with a thought. Life is a dance. Every day, we move to the rhythm of our emotions, our passions and our desires. In Lingam massage, we have found a way to express this dance, to honor and celebrate it. So why not take the next step, why not dive deeper into the abyss of human connection and discover all it has to offer? I look forward to seeing you in the next chapter, where together we'll explore the depths of emotional connection and its transformative power. You won't want to miss it.

Chapter 12: The Emotional Connection: Looks, Words and Other Ties

Have you ever felt the electricity that surges between two people when they stare into each other's eyes? That tingle that runs across the skin when they share intimate words and feelings without uttering a single word? If the answer is yes, then you know exactly what we're going to talk about in this chapter. If not, you're about to embark on an eye-opening journey that will change the way you connect with your partner.

Throughout this book we have explored the art and science behind Lingam massage, but there is one component that is often overlooked: the emotional connection. Without it, even the most expertly executed massage can feel empty or incomplete. Now, why is this important? Well, imagine building a house without a foundation. It might look impressive on the outside, but over time, it will inevitably crumble.

This emotional connection acts as the foundation of all intimate experience, and in this chapter, we will explore why it is so crucial and how to cultivate it.

To begin with, let me ask you a question: Can you remember a time when you felt such a deep emotional connection with someone that it seemed as if you were both on the same wavelength? A time when words were superfluous because you could feel exactly what the other person felt. You're probably smiling at the memory, aren't you?

This level of connection is what we all crave in our most intimate relationships. It is not something that can be forced; it must be cultivated and nurtured. And, when done correctly, it can take Lingam massage, or any other intimate experience, to heights you would never have imagined.

Now, how do we get this connection? It's not simply by staring into your partner's eyes or whispering sweet words. It is an art in itself, combining the ability to be present, to listen, and, above all, to be vulnerable.

Vulnerability. Yes, I know what you're thinking. In our society, this term is often viewed with suspicion, associated with weakness or fragility. But what if I told you that being vulnerable is actually a sign of strength? Dr. Brené Brown, in her book "Daring Greatly" (2012), states that vulnerability is at the core of all the emotions and feelings we wish to experience in life. It is the path to love, belonging and joy.

By allowing yourself to be vulnerable, you create a safe space for your partner to do the same. It is in this space that true emotional connection begins to blossom.

Now, with that foundation in place, it's time to dive into the specific techniques and practices that will allow you to establish and strengthen this connection. And as you do so, I invite you to reflect, to feel, and to dare to be vulnerable. After all, as Mark Twain said, "Life is a game best played when it is played freely."

Yes, it may sound scary at first, but I promise you the journey will be worth it. So, are you ready to dive into the depths of emotional connection and discover what it really means to be connected? Here we go.

Establishing an emotional connection may seem ethereal, but in reality, it is an art that has been studied and analyzed in depth by many experts over the years. Let's explore some of the most valuable lessons they have offered in this regard.

Renowned psychologist John Gottman, in his work "The Seven Principles for Making Marriage Work" (1999), talks about the importance of "turning toward" our partner rather than "turning away" or "turning against." But what exactly does this mean? Imagine you are sharing an experience with your partner. It could be something as simple as watching a sunset together. If at that moment your partner comments on how beautiful the sky is, you have three options: you can ignore it (turn away), you can contradict it (turn against) or you can agree and share the moment (turn toward). These small moments, according to Gottman, are the opportunities we are presented with to strengthen emotional connection.

While it is easy to understand and practice this principle in everyday situations, in the context of Lingam massage, it takes on an even deeper dimension. Every touch, every glance, every shared sigh is an opportunity to "turn towards" your partner and strengthen that connection.

On the other hand, psychoanalyst Stephen Mitchell, in "Relational Concepts in Psychoanalysis" (1988), provides insight into the role desire plays in emotional connection. According to Mitchell, desire is more than just a physical response; it is a force that drives us to connect with others on a deep and meaningful level. During Lingam massage, this desire is not only palpable, but acts as the bridge between the physical and the emotional.

Now, the art of connecting emotionally would not be complete without mentioning the importance of language. Words have the power to build or destroy. Therefore, it is essential to choose our words carefully and consciously. It is not simply what we say, but how we say it. Tone, rhythm and word choice can have a profound impact on the experience.

Remember the power of a gentle whisper in the ear, or the impact of words of affirmation that validate and celebrate the other person. These are not just words; they are verbal caresses that can deepen the emotional connection.

However, as we explore these concepts, I invite you to remember that each individual is unique. What works for one may not work for another. So, as always, I encourage you to listen, observe and feel. Emotional connection is not a destination, but an ongoing journey of discovery.

Take it slow, enjoy the process and celebrate every little advance. After all, it is through these intimate moments that we really begin to know and understand our partner. And it is in this knowledge that we find the true meaning of emotional connection.

You may find yourself asking yourself as you immerse yourself in this reading, "How can I really strengthen this emotional connection during Lingam massage?" Well, let me guide you through practical examples that can illustrate and solidify these ideas in your mind.

First, let's imagine a common situation in a couple. Roberto and Valeria, after ten years together, feel that the spark in their relationship has diminished. While they both long to rekindle that passion, they don't know exactly how to go about it. After reading about Lingam massage, Valeria decides to try it as a way to reconnect.

On the chosen day, Valeria decides to start with a quiet dinner. As they converse, she purposely remembers the importance of "turning to" Roberto. So, instead of responding with monosyllables or being distracted, she actively listens to every word he says, asking him questions and showing genuine interest.

Then, they move to a comfortable space that Valeria has prepared for the massage. Soft candlelight, quiet music and the scent of essential oils create an atmosphere that invites intimacy.

Now, Mitchell's theory comes into play. As Valeria begins the massage, she allows her desire to connect with Roberto to be the guiding force behind each touch. It is not just a series of techniques and movements; it is an expression of her desire to be close to him, to understand and love him in all his depth.

After a few minutes, Roberto, feeling Valeria's sincerity in every caress, decides to open up and share some of his insecurities. Here, Valeria remembers the importance of language and responds with words of affirmation and love. She tells him how much she values, respects and desires him.

This scene may look like something out of a romance book to you, but it is a realistic representation of what can happen when we apply what we have learned from experts like Gottman and Mitchell in the context of Lingam massage.

Of course, not every session will be like this. There will be days when connection flows easily, and others when it seems elusive. But, as Brene Brown mentions in "The Power of Being Vulnerable" (2012), "Vulnerability is the core, the heart, the center, of meaningful experiences of human connection."

And what better way to be vulnerable than through conscious touch and authentic emotional connection? So, as you move forward on this journey, I invite you to embrace vulnerability, be brave and open yourself to the endless possibilities that Lingam massage offers. Because, at the end of the day, beyond techniques and advice, it is sincerity and surrender that really makes the difference.

Within each of us, there is a deep need to feel seen, understood and connected to others. And through the practice of Lingam massage, that emotional connection becomes a bridge, a pathway to deeper mutual understanding. As the respected psychologist Carl Rogers indicated in his influential work "The Process of Becoming a Person" (1961), being truly heard and understood can be a profoundly transformative experience.

However, this connection does not end only in verbal or emotional understanding. It goes beyond, transcending the boundaries of ego, skin and mind. Have you asked yourself, how does your partner really feel? What sensations, thoughts and emotions does he or she experience during the massage? You may have felt a hint of this throughout this chapter. But that's where the beauty of the art of Lingam massage comes in.

Take, for example, a simple caress on the wrist. It may seem insignificant at first, but when that caress is imbued with intention, with a desire to connect, it becomes a message. A message that says, "I am here with you. I see you. I value you."

As you reflect on these ideas, you may feel a mixture of wonder, curiosity and even a little fear. That's natural. After all, deepening emotional connection requires courage, a commitment to let go of our defenses and open ourselves to the other's experience.

But what if I told you that this is just the tip of the iceberg? That beyond the emotional connection, there is another level of understanding and connection waiting to be explored.

As you move through this book, each chapter takes you one step closer to that understanding. And as you prepare to move into the next chapter, I encourage you to keep your mind and heart open. Because Chapter 13 will take you on a journey through the role of the receiver: surrender and trust. You will discover not only how to receive a Lingam massage, but also how to surrender to the experience, trust your partner and, most importantly, trust yourself.

So, are you ready to dive into the depths of surrender and trust? Ready to discover how these two elements can revolutionize your Lingam massage experience and, by extension, your love and sex life? If the answer is yes, take a deep breath and join me in the next chapter. Because I promise, it will be a journey you won't want to miss.

Chapter 13: The Receiver's Role: Delivery and Trust

When you think of a massage, what image comes to mind? A therapist working painstakingly while the receiver remains passive, enjoying the pleasure of the touch? But what if I told you that there is much more to the role of the receiver than meets the eye? What if the act of receiving itself is as active, as vital, as the act of giving?

Surrender and trust are two concepts that are often relegated to the background in many aspects of our lives. In a society that values self-sufficiency, independence and control, the act of surrendering, of opening up completely, can seem counterintuitive, even vulnerable. But what if that vulnerability was precisely the key to a transformative experience?

Consider this: during a Lingam massage, the recipient becomes the canvas on which the therapist draws his or her art. But what happens if that canvas becomes strained, resists or closes? The art becomes distorted, and the connection is lost. Similarly, if the canvas is surrendered, opened and trusted in the artist's hands, the result can be a masterpiece of pleasure and connection.

Have you ever stopped to consider how much trust it takes to surrender completely? To let go of your defenses and open yourself to another person, whether physically, emotionally or spiritually. It is a courageous act, an act that requires deep self-knowledge and self-acceptance.

I invite you to reflect on this. Think about the times you have resisted receiving, whether it was a compliment, help or even pleasure. What did you feel at that moment: fear, shame, doubt? Now, imagine the feeling of breaking free from those chains, of allowing yourself to receive fully, without reservation. What would that be like? What would change in your life if you could embrace that level of surrender and trust?

True vulnerability is not a weakness, but a strength," wrote Brené Brown in "The Power of Vulnerability" (2012). When we allow someone else to see our true selves, we not only show up as we really are, but we also give that person permission to do the same. It is a reciprocal exchange, a dance of give and take that allows us to connect on a deeper level.

In the context of Lingam massage, this deep connection can open doors to previously unexplored levels of pleasure and understanding. But how do we get to that point, how do we cultivate that surrender and trust? These are the questions we will explore throughout this chapter. Because, at the end of the day, the role of the receiver is as vital, as essential, as that of the giver.

And as you prepare to go deeper into this exploration, I encourage you to have an open mind and a willing heart. Because, as you will see, surrender and trust are much more than just words. They are the bridge to a richer, deeper, more connected experience.

So, are you ready to embark on this journey? Ready to discover the transformative power of surrender and trust? Take a deep breath, and step with me into this fascinating world of connection and delight. Because, as Carl Rogers would say, "When a person realizes that he or she is deeply heard and understood, he or she has the capacity to change."

There is power in the act of receiving. It is an art, a subtle balance between opening up and maintaining clear boundaries. Over the years, several authors have explored the transformative nature of receiving. In "The Art of Receiving: How to Open to Life and Others" (1998), Amanda Owen delves into the importance of receiving with grace and how this act can enhance our lives in unexpected ways.

Mentioning Owen's work is no coincidence. His ideas are especially pertinent in the context of Lingam massage. The role of the receiver becomes a conscious act of receiving, of opening oneself to pleasure, connection and spiritual experience. But how can we reach that point of total surrender, of blind trust in our partner or therapist?

Let's start with trust. Trust is not a monolithic entity; it is a mosaic composed of countless small acts, decisions and experiences. As Stephen R. Covey emphasized in "The 7 Habits of Highly Effective People" (1989), "Trust is the most essential link in every human relationship." Without trust, there can be no true connection. And in Lingam massage, connection is paramount.

So how do we build that trust? It's a combination of open communication, empathy and mutual understanding. It's being present, both physically and emotionally, for your partner or therapist. It's setting clear boundaries and respecting them, always. At the end of the day, trust is something that is earned, not automatically given.

And then there is the surrender. Oh, the beautiful, vulnerable, powerful surrender. It is not passivity, nor is it a relinquishing of control. It is a conscious act, a decision to open to experience, to let go of expectations and simply be in the moment. As Thich Nhat Hanh observed in "The Miracle of Mindfulness" (1975), "True liberation comes from deep insight, not from the desire to let go or resist."

But what does this mean in practical terms? It means focusing on the sensations, on the energy flowing between the giver and the receiver. It means letting go of distractions, fears and insecurities and simply being, fully and completely, in the present moment.

The combination of trust and surrender can transform Lingam massage from a simple physical act to a deeply spiritual and connected experience. It can open doors to previously unexplored levels of pleasure and understanding.

It is a journey, one that requires effort, introspection and, at times, overcoming personal obstacles and barriers. But isn't that the nature of all worthwhile journeys? And this, dear reader, is certainly one such journey.

So, as we continue to explore the depth and richness of the role of the receiver, I invite you to reflect on your own experiences, on the times you have fully surrendered, and the times you have resisted. Because, at the end of the day, it is in that reflection, in that self-knowledge, that true transformation is found.

Remember the first time you fully trusted someone? That feeling of letting go, of letting go of your defenses and allowing someone else to guide you? Maybe it was a friend, a therapist, or even an extreme sports instructor. In "The Power of Vulnerability" (2012), Brené Brown stresses that "Vulnerability is not winning or losing; it is having the courage to show up and be seen when we can't control the outcome."

Let's dive into some examples, so that you can further visualize the importance of surrender and trust in the Lingam massage process.

Imagine you are on a mountain, preparing for paragliding. The instructor has assured you that the equipment is safe, that you have received the proper training and that it is the perfect day to fly. However, you feel the vertigo at the edge of the cliff. Would you jump? Now, imagine that the instructor is someone you trust implicitly, someone who has flown with you many times and has demonstrated competence and care on every jump. That trust can be the difference between staying on the ground and taking to the sky.

Similarly, in Lingam massage, the role of the receiver is similar to that of the paraglider. It takes trust in the giver and in oneself to fully surrender to the experience. And when that happens, the sensations can be as high as flying.

Another example that comes to mind is that of renowned therapist Carl Rogers. In "The Process of Becoming a Person" (1961), Rogers talks about the importance of the "genuine encounter" between therapist and client, where both fully see and accept each other. It is in such an environment, where there is empathy, authenticity and unconditional acceptance, that true healing and growth occur.

Relating this to Lingam massage, the giver creates a similar space of unconditional acceptance for the receiver. In this safe space, the receiver can explore, feel and heal without judgment or expectation. It is a genuine exchange, in which both parties are fully present and connected.

You may now be asking yourself, "How do I achieve that genuine connection with my partner? How do I, as the receiver, open myself fully to the experience?" And this is where self-knowledge comes into play. Before one can give oneself to another, one must know and accept oneself. It is an inner journey, an exploration of one's own shadows, fears, desires and limits.

Think of it as a trip to an unfamiliar country. Before you embark on the adventure, you research, prepare and familiarize yourself with the terrain. In the same way, before you give yourself fully into Lingam massage, you must familiarize yourself with your own internal terrain. And don't worry, in the previous chapters we have provided tools and techniques that will help you on this journey.

So, as you continue this exploration, I encourage you to reflect on your own ability to trust and surrender, not only in Lingam massage, but in all areas of your life. Because, as we have seen, surrender and trust are fundamental to a full and connected experience. And at the end of the day, isn't that what we all seek?

Surrender and trust are not static elements; they are built and nurtured over time. As you immerse yourself in the practice of Lingam massage, these two qualities strengthen, creating an upward spiral of connection and pleasure. If we take a look at the literature on intimate relationships, we find that vulnerability, a sort of sister to surrender, is a key to deep connection. "The Seven Principles for Making Marriage Work" (1999) by John Gottman underscores the idea that shared vulnerability builds bridges between couples, strengthening their union.

Imagine for a moment a clay sculpture. At first, it is rigid, but as it is worked, it heats up and softens. In that malleable state, it can be molded into beautiful, expressive and unique shapes. Likewise, the surrender and trust in Lingam massage allows you to be shaped and molded, creating a dance of energy and pleasure that is as unique as fingerprints.

And you know what's most intriguing about all this? Every experience is different. Every time you surrender, you open yourself to new sensations, emotions and discoveries. Philosopher Alan Watts, in his book "The Way of Zen" (1957), talks about living in the present, being fully in the here and now. And that is exactly what the Lingam massage delivery invites you to do: to be fully present, feeling every caress, every breath, every wave of energy.

Now, dear reader, we have sailed together through the waters of surrender and trust, understanding its essence and its transforming power. However, like any journey, there are always higher waves to conquer, and in this case, they are the waves of excitement.

Are you ready to understand how arousal flows, how to navigate its ups and downs, and how to use it to intensify pleasure? The next chapter will immerse you in the wonderful world of arousal cycles. You will discover how to identify, understand and play with these waves, taking Lingam massage to new heights of pleasure.

So, take a deep breath, let the anticipation fill you, and dive with us into Chapter 14. We promise it will be an unforgettable journey.

Chapter 14: Navigating the Waves: Understanding Excitation Cycles

Have you ever wondered what it's like to fly - that indescribable feeling of freedom, of floating through the clouds and being carried away by the breeze? The excitement, in many ways, is comparable to that experience of flying. It's a journey where we rise and fall, glide and float, and sometimes dive deep into the ocean of desire.

Arousal is not simply a physiological response to a stimulus. It is a holistic experience involving body, mind and spirit. Now, dear reader, imagine for a moment that you have the ability to read and understand every sign of this journey, to know when it is time to ascend and when it is time to descend, to be able to take your partner (or yourself) to unimaginable heights of pleasure. Fascinating, isn't it?

But why is it so important to understand these cycles of arousal? Because by doing so, we not only enhance our sexual experience, but we also strengthen our connection and communication with our partner. We develop an attunement, a silent but powerful language that allows us to navigate together in this sea of sensations.

Think about it, isn't it amazing how a simple caress can trigger a series of reactions in the body? Or how the sound of agitated breathing can heighten our own arousal? These are all indicators of arousal cycles, and learning to recognize them is the first step to becoming a master of Lingam massage.

Sexologist William Masters and psychologist Virginia Johnson, in their landmark study "Human Sexual Response" (1966), described the phases of sexual arousal in terms of a curve. While it is true that this study focused on sexual response, the concept is perfectly applicable to Lingam massage. After all, isn't Lingam massage a way of expressing and experiencing sexuality?

Now, before you set out to discover these cycles, I want you to pause and reflect: Are you ready to embark on this journey? Are you ready to learn, to explore and, most importantly, to enjoy?

If your answer is yes, you're on the right track. And if you still have doubts, I encourage you to keep reading, because what follows will open doors to a universe of pleasure and connection that, perhaps, you didn't even know existed.

In the end, who can resist such an exciting journey? As Robert Frost said in "The Road Not Taken" (1916), taking the road less traveled can make all the difference. And this, dear reader, is just such a road.

Well, with your permission, let's get started! We are in for a fascinating ride on the waves of excitement.
Once we dive into the vast ocean of arousal, we begin to recognize patterns and rhythms. Every human being has a unique rhythm, an imprint of excitement that distinguishes him or her, but there are certain similarities that we can learn and recognize. And just as a sailor learns to read the waves and currents, we can learn to read and navigate the waves of arousal.

You may ask: How do I identify these waves? How do I know when I am on a ridge or in a valley? The answer lies in tuning in and paying attention, not only to the body, but also to the subtle signals sent to us by the mind and spirit.

Over the years, many experts have investigated and analyzed these patterns. For example, Alfred Kinsey, in "The Sexual Behavior of Man" (1948), suggests that arousal is a continuous process that can be influenced by external and internal factors. On the other hand, Shere Hite, in "The Hite Report on Male Sexuality" (1981), emphasizes the importance of understanding the emotional and psychological factors that influence arousal.

Arousal can begin with a thought, an image or a memory. Sometimes, it is a light touch, a whisper or the smell of a fragrance that triggers that rush of sensations. As arousal increases, the body responds: breathing becomes faster, skin flushes, muscles tense.

But, beyond the physical response, there is the emotional and spiritual response. It is at this level that Lingam massage shows its true power. By approaching arousal not only from a physical but also from an emotional and spiritual perspective, it creates a holistic experience that transcends the ordinary.

Let me tell you an anecdote that illustrates this. A few years ago, I had the opportunity to attend a workshop on Tantra and Lingam Massage. During one of the sessions, one of the participants, a man in his forties, shared his experience. He said that during the massage, he felt like he was riding a giant wave. At one point, he found himself on top, feeling an overwhelming euphoria. Then, the wave began to descend, and he felt pulled into a space of serenity and peace. Throughout the massage, he navigated these waves of excitement, each one different from the last, but all equally intense.

Now, what can you learn from this story? First, that excitement is not linear. It is an ebb and flow, a journey with ups and downs. Second, that every experience is unique. What one person feels during a Lingam massage may be completely different from what someone else feels.

Therefore, the key is to be present, to be open and to be willing to explore. So, dear reader, I invite you to embark on this journey, to discover your own waves and learn to masterfully navigate them. Because, at the end of the day, it is this knowledge and connection with yourself that makes Lingam massage a truly transformative experience.

Now, how can one really begin to understand and capitalize on these waves of excitement? Is there a map, a guide that can help us not only recognize them but also navigate them? The answer is yes, and with the right understanding, you can become a master of this art.

To illustrate this, think of a musician. A musician does not just play the notes written on a score, but feels and understands the music, navigating its rhythms, tonalities and nuances. Similarly, when we understand arousal and its cycles, we can "play" the body in a way that resonates deeply, creating a symphony of pleasure.

The renowned sexologist William Masters and psychologist Virginia Johnson, in their influential work "Human Sexual

Response" (1966), presented a model of sexual response that is still a reference in the field. They proposed four phases: arousal, plateau, orgasm and resolution. These phases provide a window into the patterns of arousal that occur in the body.

Excitement is that first spark, the beginning of the fire. It is the stage where everything begins to activate. The heart beats faster, breathing intensifies and energy begins to flow.

The Plateau is a prolonged phase of intense excitement. It is the time when the energy is felt, but has not yet reached its peak. It is an equilibrium, a state of waiting.

Orgasm, that peak of pleasure, is a burst of energy. It is the climax of all the accumulated tension and energy.

Finally, **Resolution** is the return to calm. It is the body and spirit assimilating and processing the experience.

While these phases are linear in their presentation, the reality is that not all individuals go through these phases in the same way or in the same order. And this is where the skill of the Lingam massage giver comes into play. By recognizing and understanding these phases, the giver can guide and navigate these waves of arousal, taking the receiver to previously unknown depths of pleasure.

Imagine for a moment being in the middle of the ocean, on a surfboard. In front of you, a series of waves is approaching. If you have the knowledge and skill, you can ride these waves with grace and mastery, experiencing a sense of exhilaration and freedom. But if you're not prepared or don't understand the nature of these waves, you may end up submerged in the water, struggling to keep your head above water.

So it is with the waves of excitement. Understanding them, respecting them and knowing how to navigate them is essential for a truly profound and transformative experience. And this is not just theory; it is something that has been practiced and perfected over millennia.

To solidify this concept, consider tantric practice. In tantra, sexual energy is taught to be a powerful force that can be used for self-discovery and enlightenment. By learning to navigate the waves of arousal, one can access states of expanded consciousness and connect deeply with the universe.

It is this deep understanding and respect for arousal that differentiates Lingam massage from any other practice. It is a journey, a dance, a sacred exchange between giver and receiver. And when approached with the right intention and the right knowledge, the results can be absolutely amazing.
Now that you have a clearer understanding of the waves of arousal and how they flow, it is essential to remember that each individual is unique. Sure, there are general patterns and phases that can be identified, but each person responds and feels differently. Have you ever wondered what it would be like to connect deeply with someone, perceive their rhythms and navigate precisely through their waves of pleasure? Lingam massage allows you to do just that.

Consider, for a moment, the great navigators of history, such as Christopher Columbus or Vasco da Gama. They did not simply set sail aimlessly; they studied maps, learned from other navigators and developed skills over many voyages.

Likewise, to become a master of Lingam massage, it is essential that you arm yourself with knowledge and practice continuously.

Psychologist Mihaly Csikszentmihalyi, in his book "Flow: A Psychology of Happiness" (1990), addresses the idea that when people are fully immersed in an activity and in a state of "flow," they experience deep satisfaction and joy. When you give yourself completely to the art of Lingam massage, you are not only providing pleasure to the receiver, but you are also entering into this state of flow, creating a transcendent experience for both of you.

The real beauty of this practice lies in the connection. It is not simply a physical act, but an energetic exchange. When you can read and navigate your partner's waves of arousal, you create a bond that goes beyond the physical, a bond that can bring you both to deeper states of ecstasy and connection than ever before.

As we look back on this chapter, we have sailed together through the vast ocean of arousal, understanding its cycles, rhythms and nuances. But what's next after that, how can we move beyond the peak of pleasure and explore as yet uncharted territory?

And this is where I invite you to continue our journey. The next chapter will take you to a dimension where pleasure merges with the spiritual. Are you ready to discover the spiritual dimension of pleasure, a place where ecstasy becomes a gateway to the divine? Because, after all, Lingam massage is not just a technique, it is a path to self-discovery and enlightenment. Move forward with me, and together we will explore territories you may never have imagined existed. The adventure has just begun.

Chapter 15: Beyond the Orgasm: The Spiritual Dimension of Pleasure

Orgasm is undoubtedly one of the most intense and pleasurable moments a human being can experience. But have you ever considered that pleasure could go beyond that fleeting instant? That, possibly, the real pleasure does not reside only in that climax, but in the whole journey that leads us to it, and even in what comes after.

However, before we dive into the deep waters of the spiritual dimension of pleasure, let me ask you: What does spirituality mean to you? Is it perhaps a connection to something greater than oneself? A link to the universe, to energy, to the divine? Or perhaps it is simply a deep sense of inner peace and harmony? Take a moment to reflect on these questions. Feel within yourself the resonance they may have, and give yourself permission to explore your own definition of spirituality.

Modern culture often separates spirituality from sexuality, as if they were mutually exclusive entities. But what if I told you that in ancient traditions, such as Tantra, sexuality and spirituality were seen as two sides of the same coin? In these traditions, sexual energy is not simply a tool for physical pleasure, but also a gateway to a deeper, transcendental experience.

To illustrate this, let's think of a fire. Fire can be a source of heat and light, providing comfort and visibility. But, at the same time, if we get too close without care, we can get burned. In the same way, our sexual energy can be a source of pleasure and connection, but it also has the potential to bring you to a state of spiritual ecstasy, if you know how to handle and channel it properly.

The renowned author Joseph Campbell, in his work "The Hero with a Thousand Faces" (1949), talks about the importance of the heroic journey, how the hero embarks on an adventure, faces challenges and finally returns transformed. This metaphor can be perfectly applied to the journey of pleasure. The sexual experience, particularly Lingam massage, can be a heroic journey into self-discovery, into merging with the energy of the universe. Isn't it exciting to think that every intimate encounter has the potential to be an odyssey into the unknown, an exploration of self and other?

Laughter is often the best medicine, and in this journey, humor is essential. Imagine for a moment that orgasm is like a joke. The anticipation, the foreplay, is the beginning of the joke, the development of the story. The orgasm is the punch line, the uncontrollable laughter that ensues. But what happens after laughing? There remains a feeling of lightness, of joy. Such is the spiritual dimension of pleasure, that echo that resounds after the orgasm, that lightness that is felt after the laughter.

So, as you embark on this journey into the spiritual dimension of pleasure, I invite you to open yourself to the possibilities. To see beyond the obvious and discover the mysteries that the connection between body and spirit can reveal. As mentioned in Chapter 13, surrender and trust are essential in this process. So, relax, take a deep breath and let yourself be carried by the current of this river of ancient wisdom. For, after all, this journey is as old as humanity itself.

Tantra, which we have already discussed, has been one of the most influential traditions in connecting the sexual and the spiritual. And, as we navigate deeper into this connection, it is critical to understand that, despite different cultural and religious interpretations, the basis of Tantra is the idea that everything in the universe is interconnected.

If you stop for a moment and close your eyes, you can imagine a vast web stretching in all directions. Each point of this web represents a being, an object, an idea. And each connection, an energetic link that unites us all. This web is the manifestation of universal energy. And, when we connect with our own pleasure and elevate it to the spiritual plane, we are actually touching this universal energy, expanding and sharing it.

Margot Anand, in her influential work "The Art of Sexual Ecstasy" (1995), stresses that our sexuality is a doorway to spiritual expansion. Pleasure is not just a physical response to a stimulus, but a reverberation of our connection to the whole. It is a response to our identity in relation to the universe. This idea, although it may seem abstract at first, makes sense when we consider that every cell in our body vibrates and responds to the energies around it.

Now, take a moment to reflect: When was the last time you felt that vibration, that connection, not only with your partner, but with everything around you? Have you noticed how after a really meaningful intimate moment, everything seems brighter, more vibrant? That's the energy we're talking about. It's not just a chemical reaction in your brain, it's a communion with the universe.

Within the Tantric tradition, sexual union is seen as a form of yoga, a method of uniting individual consciousness with universal consciousness. Just as in yoga, postures and breathing techniques are practiced to align the body and spirit, in Tantra, and particularly in Lingam massage, we use pleasure as a tool to reach higher states of consciousness.

Don't forget that, as in any journey, there are challenges. You might encounter internal barriers, limiting beliefs or simply fear of the unknown. But isn't fear often an indication that we are on the verge of something big? Doesn't that make you feel, somehow, more alive?

Sex, pleasure and spirituality are so intertwined that often when one expands, so do the others. Imagine a symphony: each instrument brings its own tone, and when they all come together, they create sublime music. In the same way, when you connect with your own pleasure and elevate it to a spiritual dimension, you create a symphony in your life, a music that resonates not only within you, but throughout the universe. It is a transformative experience, one that invites you to see the world, and yourself, from a whole new perspective. It is a journey worth taking, not only for the pleasure that awaits you, but for the deep connection with the whole that it offers.

The connection between pleasure and the spiritual is not a new or isolated concept. Throughout history, many cultures have recognized the vital and transformative energy that resides in sexual union. But how can one truly experience this transcendent dimension of pleasure?

A tangible example that can help us understand this is that of Kundalini. In Hinduism, Kundalini is described as an energy found at the base of the spine. When awakened, this energy ascends through the chakras or energy centers of the body, leading the experiencer to higher states of consciousness. It is no coincidence that many of the symptoms described when experiencing Kundalini awakening are similar to those of orgasm: a feeling of electricity, warmth, a surge of ascending energy. It is the convergence of body and spirit, the ecstasy that connects us with the whole.

Now, if you are wondering how to achieve this, consider the following anecdote by George Feuerstein in his book "The Tantric Tradition" (2003). He tells the story of a monk who, upon reaching spiritual ecstasy during meditation, described the experience as "ten thousand simultaneous orgasms." Can you imagine? A pleasure so profound and overwhelming that it surpasses any previously known experience.

However, you don't need to be a monk or retreat to a cave in the Himalayas to experience this. The conscious practice of Lingam massage, for example, can be a path to that transcendental connection. By focusing on pleasure and opening to sexual energy, you become more receptive to the spiritual energy flowing through you. By learning to channel this energy, you can elevate your sexual experiences to a higher plane, connecting to a source of energy that goes beyond the physical.

For many, this connection is experienced as a feeling of oneness. I remember a testimony from Samuel, a man who practiced Lingam massage with his partner after reading Chapter 9. He wrote to me telling me how, in a moment of deep pleasure, he felt that he and his partner merged, that there were no longer any boundaries between their bodies. He felt that they were part of something bigger, of an energy that encompassed and transcended them.

Have you ever felt that sensation of floating, of being one with everything, even for a brief moment during lovemaking? If so, you've had a glimpse of what the spiritual dimension of pleasure is all about. And if you haven't experienced it yet, don't worry. With the right guidance and an open mind and heart, it's an experience within everyone's reach.

And this is where the value of self-knowledge and self-exploration comes into play, which we will talk more about in Chapter 25. For, at the end of the day, everyone has their own unique path to spiritual connection. What works for one may not work for another. But the journey, with its ups and downs, discoveries and revelations, is what really matters.
Our journey through the spiritual dimension of pleasure has revealed the depths that exist beyond the simple physical act. It is fascinating to think that, within every human being, lies an energy waiting to be awakened and channeled toward elevation and transcendence.

It is worth quoting Anais Nin, an author who wrote masterfully about the complexities of desire and love in her diary published in 1966. She said, "We do not reach orgasm because we restrict ourselves. Living to the fullest includes pain." In this quote, Nin recognizes that to truly experience pleasure at its peak, one must be willing to embrace all facets of the human experience, including pain.

Lingam massage, in its highest practice, becomes a tool that transcends physical pleasure and enters the spiritual realm. It is a means to release blockages, heal wounds and reconnect with the divine source that resides in each of us. But, as with any spiritual practice, it requires dedication, patience and, above all, the right intention.

You may be asking yourself, "What now, how do I integrate all of this into my daily life?". Well, that's the beauty of this journey: it has no final destination. It is an ongoing process of discovery and evolution.

As you recall what we have explored in this chapter, reflect on how the spiritual dimension of pleasure can enrich your life and your relationships. Consider how, by embracing this dimension, you can experience a deeper connection not only with your partner, but with yourself and the universe at large.

Now then, as we close this chapter and you prepare to embark on the next, I offer you a promise: Chapter 16 will guide you through solutions to common challenges in Lingam massage. Not everything is a bed of roses, and it is essential to be prepared to face and overcome any obstacles that come your way. Have you encountered challenges or doubts while practicing? Are there aspects of Lingam massage that you still find perplexing or intimidating? If so, the next chapter will be essential for you. It will offer you tools, techniques and tips to overcome these challenges and ensure an enriching and transformative experience for both participants.

So, I invite you to move forward, to continue exploring and discovering. The beauty of this journey is in every step you take, in every revelation and in every deep connection you make. See you in the next chapter, where we will continue to unravel the mysteries of Lingam Massage and its power to transform our lives.

Chapter 16: Solutions to Common Challenges in Lingam Massage

In a world full of manuals, tutorials and guides for everything, you may be asking yourself, why isn't there a clear solution to every Lingam massage challenge? The reality is that while there are standard practices and techniques, the real magic lies in the ability to adapt, to learn and to grow with each experience. But that doesn't mean you are alone in this journey.

Now, I propose a pause. Take a deep breath. Imagine a road full of rocks, highs and lows, some moments sunny and others cloudy. As you go along, you face obstacles, but each one teaches you something new, shapes you, transforms you. Do you remember a situation where you faced a challenge and overcame it and felt stronger, more capable? This chapter is exactly that: a compass to help you navigate through the shifting currents of Lingam massage.

Why is it so essential to face and overcome challenges in this practice? Simple. Lingam massage, like any other practice that involves the intimate connection between two human beings, is not an exact science. It is a dance, an exchange of energy, a constant flow of give and take. And with that flow comes inevitable challenges, learning and opportunities for growth.

Have you ever stopped to think about the fears and blocks that may arise during this type of massage? Or how your partner may feel insecure, vulnerable or even intimidated by the intensity of the experience? These are just some of the challenges that can arise. And it's only natural. After all, we are exploring often uncharted territory, plunging into the depths of pleasure and human connection.

The great author and philosopher Alan Watts, in his work "The Way of Zen" (1957), mentioned how facing the unknown and the uncertain opens the door to a greater understanding and connection with the world around us. He said: "To discover what we do not know, we must venture on the path of uncertainty". And in uncertainty, in vulnerability, lie opportunities to deepen our understanding, to grow and transform ourselves.

As we move into this chapter, I invite you to open your mind and heart. Allow yourself to feel, question and explore. Allow yourself to be vulnerable. And remember, every challenge you face is an opportunity to grow, to learn, and to connect more deeply with your partner and yourself.

Therefore, as you embark on this journey through Chapter 16, I encourage you to approach each challenge with curiosity, with love, and with the certainty that you are on the right path to a richer and deeper experience of Lingam massage. After all, as we mentioned in Chapter 3, the anatomy of pleasure is a universe unto itself, and each challenge is simply a star waiting to be discovered.

And now, if you're ready, let's delve into solutions to these common challenges. Because every stone in the path can become a stepping stone to success. I will guide you step by step, with the same love and care with which one practices Lingam massage. Are you ready for the journey?

So, as you move along this path, you're likely to encounter challenges that at first glance seem insurmountable. But have you considered that these challenges might actually be opportunities in disguise? Let's look at some of the most common challenges and how to overcome them with grace and confidence.

One of the first and most recurring challenges is lack of communication. Lingam massage, being such an intimate practice, requires open and honest communication between the giver and receiver. Communication is the cornerstone of any intimate experience. Remember the last time you felt misunderstood or unable to express your wants and needs? Yes, it's not a pleasant feeling. Now, multiply that feeling tenfold when it is such an intimate and vulnerable experience.

Marguerite Duras, in her masterful work "The Lover" (1984), explored the depths and complexities of communication and human connection. She expressed that "the word is a bridge between two souls". And that is exactly what we seek here: to build bridges of connection through communication. Therefore, it is essential that the giver asks, listens and adapts to the needs of the receiver. And vice versa. Active listening is key in this process.

Another common challenge is expectation. In our society, we are programmed to look for results, to reach goals. However, in Lingam massage, the process is more important than the destination. If you focus solely on achieving a certain result, such as bringing on an orgasm, you will miss the beauty and depth of the whole process. Eckhart Tolle, in "The Power of Now" (1997), reminded us that true power lies in the present, in the "here and now". And in Lingam massage, it is essential that you immerse yourself completely in the present moment, freeing yourself from expectations and enjoying every sensation, every touch, every connection.

What about emotional disconnection? This is another challenge many people face. You may find yourself giving or receiving the massage, but your mind is somewhere else, caught up in worries or distractions. Here, mindfulness practice can be your best ally. Mindfulness, as Jon Kabat-Zinn taught us in "Wherever You Go, There You Are" (1994), is the ability to be fully present, aware of where we are and what we are doing, without reacting to or feeling overwhelmed by what is going on around us.

Ultimately, what these challenges have in common is a lack of connection, either with oneself or with one's partner. And overcoming these challenges is essential to getting the most out of the Lingam massage experience.

So I invite you, as you face these challenges, to see them not as obstacles, but as opportunities. Opportunities to grow, to learn, to connect more deeply. Each challenge is an open door to a new level of understanding and connection. And with the right tools and techniques, each of these obstacles becomes a valuable lesson. But before we dive into the solution, let me tell you a story that perfectly illustrates how to face challenges in Lingam massage.

Once upon a time in a small village in India, there was a tantric master named Ananda. He was known in faraway regions for his ability to teach and practice the art of Lingam massage. Many came from far and wide to learn from him. One evening, a young disciple named Arjun approached him with concern on his face.

Master," Arjun began, "every time I try to practice massage, my partner feels uncomfortable or anxious. I feel lost and don't know how to overcome this challenge."

Ananda, with a serene smile, asked him, "Arjun, when the river finds a rock in its path, what does it do?"

The disciple, a little confused, replied, "It flows around you, master."

Exactly," Ananda replied. "He doesn't fight the rock, nor does he try to move it. Just find a new path and keep flowing. You must be like the river, Arjun. If you encounter resistance or discomfort, don't fight it. Just adapt your approach and keep flowing."

This story highlights the importance of adaptability and flexibility in our practice. Each person is unique and what works for one may not be right for another.

But back to our challenges: How can we, in practical terms, address and overcome these barriers? Let's look at some concrete examples.

Challenge 1: Lack of Communication. Solution: In addition to active listening, create a safe space where both parties can express their needs, fears and desires without judgment. As Brené Brown teaches us in "The Power of Being Vulnerable" (2012), vulnerability is the cradle of innovation, creativity and change.

Challenge 2: Expectations. Solution: Before starting the massage, set clear intentions, but not specific goals. Lingam massage is a journey and, as mentioned in Chapter 14, it is essential to understand arousal cycles and know that each journey is unique.

Challenge 3: Emotional disconnection. Solution: Practice mindfulness exercises together before you begin. You can try mindful breathing or guided meditation, techniques explored in detail in Chapter 6.

And so, by facing each challenge with empathy, understanding and the right tools, you will find yourself in a position of power and confidence. Each obstacle will become an opportunity to deepen the connection and enhance the experience.

After all, in the words of the Persian poet Rumi in the 13th century: "The obstacle in the path becomes the path. Never forget, within every obstacle lies an opportunity to improve our condition."

As you remember this, I invite you to keep flowing, adapting and learning. And as you continue this journey, you will find that each challenge brings you closer to the true essence and magic of Lingam massage.

In the challenges we have analyzed and the solutions we have explored, we see that there is one constant: the need for presence, for being fully immersed in the moment, and for welcoming each experience with an open mind and a willing heart. The biggest barriers are often in our minds, and overcoming them allows us to access deeper levels of connection and pleasure.

The acclaimed author, T. Harv Eker, in his work "The Secrets of the Millionaire Mind" (2005), did not talk about Lingam Massage, but he did present a universal idea: thought patterns determine our experience of life. When we shift our focus from "Why is this happening to me?" to "What can I learn from this?", we transform our challenges into powerful tools for personal growth.

It is imperative to understand that this journey is not only about technique, but also about discovery. Not just about giving, but also about receiving. Not just about pleasure, but also about connection.

To add a touch of levity, I am reminded of a humorous saying that, while it may seem irreverent, has an underlying truth: "If on the first try you don't succeed, skydiving is not for you." However, in the world of Lingam massage, you are blessed to try, learn, adapt and try again. With each attempt, you become wiser, more connected and ultimately more capable.

So what's next after mastering these challenges? Well, there is territory waiting to be explored, territory that is often overlooked but powerful and transformative. In the next chapter, we will venture into the realm of prostate massage, an experience that has the potential to take male pleasure to dizzying heights. Are you ready to dive into a sea of unknown sensations and discover hidden secrets of male pleasure? I promise you, what's to come will change your perspective and expand your repertoire in ways you can barely imagine now. So, take a deep breath, keep an open mind and join me in the next chapter, where the journey gets even more exciting.

Chapter 17: Prostatic Massage: An unknown but powerful territory

Entering the world of prostate massage may at first seem like diving into an unexplored ocean. Why, you may ask, has this most intimate and powerful aspect of male pleasure remained in the shadows for so long? Is it not a treasure waiting to be discovered, a facet of ecstasy that adds depth and dimension to the landscape of bliss?

Well, let me take you by the hand on this journey, so that you can discover for yourself the answers to these questions. But first, have you reflected on the pioneering nature of your curiosity? It is interesting how the desire to know and explore can become a powerful compass that directs us on the journey of self-discovery.

Throughout history, pleasure has been the object of scrutiny, mysticism and, at times, rejection. But, as Jordan O'Connell mentions in his work "The Rites of Ecstasy" (1998), "Pleasure is a fundamental part of being human, an inexhaustible source of self-discovery and personal evolution". So why refuse to explore all its dimensions?

The prostate, often referred to as the "male G-spot," is a gland found in the male reproductive system. Its potential in the realm of pleasure is widely underestimated. And this is where we get into the heart of the matter. How is it possible that something so intrinsically linked to male pleasure has largely remained off our radar?

Ask yourself a question: How much of what you think you know about the body and pleasure comes from true lived experience and how much from myths and misinformation? Are you willing to challenge those myths and embark on a journey of discovery? If your answer is yes, this chapter will become your star map.

Prostate massage is not simply a technique; it is an invitation. An invitation to go deeper, to connect, to discover new levels of pleasure and understanding. But to really understand its power, it is essential to get rid of prejudices and fears. Just as Lingam massage, which we discussed in the previous chapters, focuses on deep, conscious connection, prostate massage challenges us to explore a region of the body that can be a source of profound pleasure and healing.

But there's a dilemma here, isn't there? The idea of exploring prostate massage can arouse mixed feelings. Is it normal to be curious? Is it safe? What will others say? What if I discover that I really enjoy it?

Let's address each of these concerns, but first, let me pause and remind you of something: The real journey is not outward, but inward. In the words of renowned sex therapist Julia Verner in "The Nuances of Desire" (2011), "Self-discovery is the key that unlocks all the doors to pleasure."

With this in mind, and before you dive deeper into this chapter, I invite you to take a deep breath, open your mind and heart, and embark on this journey with the certainty that each step you take will bring you closer to a deeper understanding of yourself and the vast universe of male pleasure.

Prostate massage, like many aspects of pleasure, has been shrouded in layers of myth and mystery over the years. But if we go back in time, we find that history has a rich tapestry of traditions and rituals that celebrate the orgasmic potential of this small but mighty gland.

Anthony Laurent, in his groundbreaking book "The Alchemy of Pleasure" (2005), talks about how ancient civilizations, from the Mayans to the Chinese, recognized the energetic and spiritual potential of the prostate. Through rituals and massage techniques, these peoples connected with a source of power and vitality that allowed them to channel their sexual energy towards healing and transcendence.

If you're feeling a little skeptical about the power of prostate massage, you're not alone. It's natural to feel this way, especially when we venture into unfamiliar territory. But have you considered the possibility that those feelings of doubt and skepticism are more rooted in the unknown than in objective reality? For a moment, close your eyes and think back to the first time you heard about Lingam massage. Remember that mixture of curiosity and wariness?

As Camila Stratford rightly mentions in "The Limits of Pleasure" (2013), "Human beings tend to fear the unknown, but true growth happens when we face those fears and challenge them." Now, imagine a space where you can explore freely, without judgment, without fear, just with an open mind and willingness to discover.

Prostate massage, when practiced with respect, knowledge and care, can offer a number of both physical and emotional benefits. Not only can it enhance pleasure and orgasm, but it can also aid in prostate health and improve blood circulation in the pelvic area.

What if I told you there was more? Beyond the physical benefits, this type of massage can be a powerful tool for emotional and spiritual connection. But how is it possible that something so physical can have such a profound impact on our emotions and spirituality?

This is where the concept of energy comes into play. If you recall from Chapter 6, we talked about breath and energy and how these can be used to deepen the connection during Lingam massage. Similarly, prostate massage, by stimulating and activating the flow of energy in the pelvic area, can release emotional blockages and allow energy to flow freely throughout the body.

Think of it as a river. If there are obstacles or blockages in its path, the water cannot flow easily. But once these blockages are removed, the water flows freely, nourishing everything in its path. In the same way, prostate massage can help release those emotional and energetic blockages, allowing energy to flow and rejuvenate your whole being.

It's fascinating, isn't it? If you feel this journey is for you, read on. Because in the next sections, I will take you by the hand through the techniques, the benefits and everything you need to know to embark on this journey of self-discovery and pleasure.

As we continue to delve deeper into this exploration, we can't leave out the concrete examples that demonstrate the power and impact of prostate massage on people's lives. After all, there is something profoundly revealing in real-life stories, and these anecdotes can provide invaluable insight into your own journey.

Take, for example, the story of Roberto. A 45-year-old businessman who, after facing a series of health problems, decided to look for alternative ways to improve his well-being. Through a friend, Roberto was introduced to the world of tantric massage and, although skeptical at first, decided to give it a try. What he experienced during his first session was, in his own words, "a revelation, as if I had discovered a whole universe inside me that I had been ignoring all my life."

But what made Roberto's experience so transformative? One of the main techniques his therapist used during the session was prostate massage. Through a combination of deep breathing, emotional connection and gentle stimulation, Roberto was able to release accumulated tensions and connect with a source of pleasure and energy he had never experienced before.

Renowned sexologist Dr. Samuel Oliver, in his book "The Map of Male Pleasure" (1998), highlights that "The male body, especially in areas such as the prostate, harbors energy points that, when properly activated, can trigger experiences of deep ecstasy and spiritual connection." And, as Roberto discovered, these types of experiences can have a transformative impact not only on our sex lives, but on our mental and emotional health.

While each experience is unique, there are certain common elements that many people describe when experiencing a deeply connected prostate massage. The feeling of release, the perception of a flow of energy throughout the body, and a sense of wholeness and connection with oneself are some of the most recurring experiences.

Now, imagine for a moment that you are in a quiet, serene room. The light is soft, the music is soothing, and you are fully present in the moment. You feel a surge of anticipation as you prepare to receive a prostate massage. How do you feel? What emotions emerge? Let your mind dive into this scenario and feel all that comes with it. The connection, the vulnerability, the excitement, and the potential for pleasure like you've never experienced before.

You may now be asking yourself, how can I bring this imagined experience into reality? The answer lies in knowledge, practice and, most importantly, connection with yourself and your therapist or partner. In the next sections, I will offer you practical tools and specific techniques that will help you embark on this adventure of pleasure and discovery. The shadows of the past and the uncertainties of the present fade away when you connect with the innermost essence of your being. Throughout this chapter, we have ploughed uncharted seas and unraveled deep mysteries about prostate massage. Do you feel curiosity stirring inside you, yearning to explore even more?

Before concluding this journey, let us delve into the words of the renowned French tantric therapist, Laurent Dupont, who in his work "Rebirth through Tantra" (2002), wrote: "The discovery of one's own body is a journey of no return. Once one has experienced the fullness of being, one can no longer, nor does one want to, turn back." This statement resonates with potency. The search for pleasure and connection is not an end in itself, but the beginning of a journey of self-discovery.

Like any journey, there will be moments of challenge and bewilderment, but also of joy and revelation. Are you willing to embark on this journey, to shed your prejudices and open yourself to the unknown?

It is interesting to reflect on how Western culture has relegated certain parts of the body to obscurity, labeling them as taboo. However, in doing so, what treasures have we left undiscovered? In ancient Tantric traditions, every part of the body is revered as a temple, a portal to the infinite. And now, dear reader, you too are beginning the journey to those inner temples.

While we have covered a lot of ground in this chapter, there is still a vast universe to discover. Every page, every word, is designed to take you further into a deeper understanding of yourself and the possibilities of pleasure and connection that lie within.

So, do you dare to continue? In the next chapter, we will unveil "The multiple facets of the male orgasm". Dare to dive into the ocean of male pleasure in all its variations and dimensions. It will be a journey that, I promise, will transform your perspective on sexuality and pleasure. With each page you turn, a new horizon will open up before you, full of secrets and surprises that will change your life forever. So why wait? The adventure awaits you on the next page.

Chapter 18: The many facets of the male orgasm

Have you ever felt, dear reader, that there is a gulf of ignorance as to the nuances and varieties of the male orgasm? In the most intimate spheres of our culture, it has long been assumed that the male orgasm is simple, straightforward, a straight line to a predictable end. But what if I told you that this perception is, for the most part, a gross oversimplification?

First, it is vital to understand that male sexuality, like female sexuality, is vast and complex. It is a mosaic of sensations, emotions and connections that goes beyond the mere physical act. And, like all art, it requires appreciation and understanding. How often have we heard that men are "simple" in their desires and responses? But is this really so, or have we been closing our minds and hearts to a deeper understanding?

Let's start by understanding why this topic is important. Sexual fulfillment is not just about pleasure; it is a route to self-discovery, self-acceptance and, ultimately, deep connection with oneself and one's partner. By limiting our understanding of the male orgasm to a simple release of energy, we are depriving ourselves of the rich tapestry of experiences and connections it can offer.

As you immerse yourself in these words, you may find yourself wondering: What have I overlooked? What wonders, sensations and emotions are there, waiting to be discovered and explored? How can this knowledge enrich my life or that of my partner?

Recall what we mentioned in *Chapter 3: Anatomy of Pleasure: Discovering the Male Universe*. In it, we unpacked the complexities of the male body and its capacity for pleasure. Now, in this chapter, we will go a step further, delving into the heart of the male orgasm, unraveling its mysteries and revealing its many facets.

Perhaps some of you are familiar with Desmond Morris' work, "The Naked Ape" (1967). Morris, in his research, suggests that the human sexual response is much more than a mere reflex. It is a dialogue between body and mind, a dance between desire and response. And, as in any dance, there are rhythms, movements and steps that, when understood and practiced, can take the act to the next level.

But what if the key lies in the questions we ask ourselves? Questions like: What is the nature of my orgasm, are there different types of orgasms I can experience, and how can I cultivate and explore these different facets in myself or in my partner?

So, I invite you to embark on this journey of exploration and discovery. Get ready to challenge preconceived notions, to look beyond the obvious, and to dive into the depths of male pleasure like never before. And who knows, maybe by the end of this chapter, your understanding of the male orgasm will no longer be the same. Are you ready? Because the journey is about to begin.

Let us now enter a terrain that has been explored by many, but which few have really understood in its entirety. In "The Function of Orgasm" (1927), Wilhelm Reich tells us about orgone energy, a type of vital energy that, according to him, is released during orgasm. And although this concept has been the subject of controversy, what we cannot deny is that there is something deeper and more energetic at play at the moment of climax. But what exactly is it?

Imagine for a moment that the male orgasm is like a symphony. It is not just an instrument playing at full volume, but an orchestra of sensations, emotions and responses that play together in perfect harmony. At the instant of orgasm, there is a culmination, a peak, but there is also a series of movements and notes leading up to that moment.

Dr. Beverly Whipple, in her book "The Science of Orgasm" (2006), discusses the various physiological and chemical responses that occur in the body during orgasm. From oxytocin release to muscle contractions, each response is a piece of the puzzle that makes up the male orgasm.

Now, if we have established that there are different "notes" and "movements" in this symphony, the question arises: How does each one feel? Is it possible to experience different types of orgasms? Some studies suggest that it is. For example, prostatic orgasm, which we have already discussed in *Chapter 17: Prostate Massage: An Uncharted but Powerful Territory*, is a very different response to the orgasm generated by lingam stimulation.

And then there are the emotional and psychological dimensions of orgasm. As Marnia Robinson states in Cupid's

Poisoned Arrow (2009), orgasm is not only a release of sexual energy, but also an emotional release. In other words, it can be a profoundly healing and transformative experience.

You may be asking yourself, "How can I begin to explore these different facets of orgasm in myself or with my partner?" Well, here's an idea: instead of focusing solely on the climax, try focusing on the journey. As with any journey, there are sights, sensations and discoveries worth exploring. Next time you're in an intimate moment, take a moment to tune into every sensation, every emotion. What will you discover?

Of course, as with any journey of discovery, it is helpful to have a guide. There are many experts in the field of sexuality who have written extensively on the subject. You may want to consult the works of authors such as Mantak Chia, author of "The Multi-Orgasmic Man" (2002), which offers techniques and exercises for cultivating different types of orgasms.

Ultimately, the male orgasm is a doorway to a world of possibilities. A world where pleasure, connection and transformation go hand in hand. A world waiting to be discovered. So, are you ready to explore? Because this journey has just begun.

Now, let's delve even deeper into this fascinating terrain. The depths of male pleasure extend far beyond simple physical release. While biology plays a fundamental role, it is the mind and soul that often become the true protagonists of this orchestra of ecstasy.

Barbara Keesling, in "How to Make Love All Night" (1994), reminds us that the male sexual experience is not merely a reflex response. It is an interplay between mind, body and spirit. And it is in this trifecta that we find the true gems of the male orgasm.

Imagine for a moment: a painter in front of his canvas, with an infinite palette of colors at his disposal. Some colors are bright and vivid, others are subtle and nuanced. The male orgasm is similar. It is not just a black and white brushstroke; it is a rainbow of sensations and emotions.

For example, think of the experience of "dry orgasm," a feeling of ecstasy without ejaculation. Here, energy is displaced upward, rather than being released outward. It is a sensation that, according to some Tantra practitioners, can be even more intense and long-lasting than the conventional orgasm. This concept is also supported by Chia in "The Multi-Orgasmic Man," where he highlights how men can learn to separate orgasm from ejaculation and experience multiple peaks of pleasure.

Next, let's take a look at the experience of prolonged orgasm. While orgasm typically lasts only a few seconds, there are those who claim they can extend that sensation for minutes, and even hours. Here, breathing and meditation play a crucial role, as does the ability to fully immerse oneself in the present moment. The power of the mind is immense and, when properly channeled, can transform the orgasmic experience into something entirely new.

But what about those moments when orgasm has a bittersweet taste? Sometimes, climax is accompanied by unexpected emotions, such as sadness or longing. These moments provide us with an invaluable opportunity to reflect and connect with our deepest emotions. It is not uncommon for men to discover old wounds or traumas during these moments of vulnerability. Pleasure and pain are intrinsically linked, and exploring this delicate balance can be profoundly healing.

To illustrate, let's think of an experience shared by Alex Comfort in "The Joy of Sex" (1972). It tells of a man who, after years of searching for the perfect orgasm, finally realizes that true pleasure lies in connection and vulnerability. It is in this space that the true jewels of male pleasure are found.

Therefore, as we navigate these depths, it is crucial to remember that the male orgasm is both a journey and a destination. Every experience, every sensation, every emotion is an opportunity to learn and grow. And while the route to ecstasy may vary from man to man, the potential for discovery and transformation is universal. Are you willing to dive in? Because, trust me, the journey is worth it.

So, dear reader, as we delve into the depths of this vast ocean of male orgasm, we find the undeniable truth that pleasure has as many facets as there are stars in the night sky. It is not just an ephemeral moment, but an expansive experience that branches out in infinite directions.

The beauty of this exploration lies in the ability to tailor and mold these experiences to perfection for each individual. Because, like an artist in front of a blank canvas, you have the freedom to create your masterpiece of pleasure. What if I told you that this is just the beginning?

Now, let me share a revealing perspective. In "The Erotic Mind" (1995), Jack Morin talks about the "ecstasy equation," where he suggests that the key to intense sexual satisfaction lies in the ability to balance safety with novelty. Imagine a balance: on one side, all that is familiar and comfortable; and on the other, the thrill of the unknown. As you enter into this dance between the known and the new, you will discover aspects of your sexuality that you never imagined.

The road to self-discovery is a winding one, and yes, at times it can seem challenging. But, as Mihaly Csikszentmihalyi rightly pointed out in "Flow: The Psychology of Optimal Experience" (1990), the most rewarding moments in life often arise when we challenge ourselves. When we dare to explore, to try, to learn.

So what comes next on this journey? Well, the next chapter will take us on a journey through time and space, exploring ancient and modern rituals. We will discover how different cultures have understood and honored the art of male pleasure. I promise, it will be a fascinating and enriching odyssey that will provide you with tools and techniques to take your experience to the next level.

Think of it this way: If this chapter was an inner journey, the next one will be an outer journey, where you'll discover that, despite cultural and temporal differences, there are common threads that connect us all in our quest for ecstasy. Are you ready to continue this journey? Because I guarantee that what comes next is so exciting and revealing that you won't want to miss it.

And, at the end of the day, the most important thing to remember is that this book is more than words on a page; it is an invitation to explore, to learn, to feel and to connect. An invitation to explore, to learn, to feel and to connect. Will you accept the challenge? Then let's move forward together into the next chapter and discover the wonders that await you there. I promise you, it will be an adventure you will never forget.

Chapter 19: Ancient and Modern Rituals: Traditions from Different Cultures

Have you ever wondered how ancient cultures approached the art of male pleasure? How have these practices transformed over time and how do they compare to the modern techniques we have discussed so far in this book? Indeed, on this stage of our journey together, we will embark on a journey through time and space, discovering how different civilizations have revered, perfected and adapted Lingam massage.

The importance of this study lies in understanding the evolution of male pleasure over the centuries. Observing the past allows us to understand and appreciate the roots of the techniques we employ today. It also gives us the opportunity to reintroduce forgotten practices and merge the ancient with the modern for a truly transformative experience.

Now, dear reader, I want you to imagine our ancestors, under the starry blanket of a night sky, practicing sacred rituals in honor of the masculine creative power, feel the earth beneath their feet, listen to the whispers of the wind, perceive the perfume of the oils and herbs used in those rituals. Feel the earth beneath your feet, listen to the whispers of the wind, smell the perfume of the oils and herbs used in those rituals. Do you feel connected to them? Do you feel a kind of déjà vu, as if you were part of a legacy much older than you?

It's curious how, as we travel through different times and places, we find similar patterns that transcend borders and time. From the ancient tantric rituals of India, to the esoteric practices of Chinese dynasties, to the erotic customs of Mesoamerican civilizations, all share a reverence for the power, energy and mystery of the male organ.

Now, you may be asking yourself, "How have these traditions influenced the practice of Lingam massage as we know it today?" The answer, my friend, will surprise you and inspire you to experiment with a new perspective, based on ancient wisdom.

And here enters a crucial reflection. Humanity, since time immemorial, has searched for ecstasy, that instant of divine connection, and to find it, it has resorted to various methods, sometimes mysterious and esoteric. To find it, we have resorted to various methods, sometimes mysterious and esoteric. Have you ever wondered why? Perhaps, in the depths of our being, we have recognized that through pleasure we can touch the divine, connect with a reality that transcends the mundane.

Think about this: if Lingam massage, as we have explored in previous chapters (referring especially to Chapter 1 and 2), is an age-old technique, what deeper meaning can it hold? What secrets, as yet unrevealed, await us in the pages of history?

As you continue with this reading, I invite you to open your mind and heart. Accept this opportunity to learn not only about techniques and methods, but also about the essence and soul of these ancient practices. For, as T.S. Eliot said, "At the end of all our exploring, we will come to the place where we began and know that place for the first time."

So, prepare your senses and your spirit. What follows is a deep immersion into rituals, secrets and wisdoms that have survived the passage of time, waiting to be rediscovered by you. Because remember, you are part of this legacy, and the power to transform and evolve this knowledge is now in your hands.

Over the centuries, various cultures have left traces of their rituals and practices surrounding Lingam massage. As we walk this path of discovery, we encounter a rich and diverse tapestry of traditions that, while they may appear different at first glance, share a common core of understanding and respect for masculine power.

Imagine, if you will, the ancient Egyptians on the banks of the Nile River. For them, sexuality was not just a biological function, but a spiritual rite that connected the earthly with the divine. In fact, Osiris, the god of life and resurrection, was associated with phallic rituals symbolizing fertility and creation. These rites often included massages and ointments made with sacred herbs and oils, designed to increase vital energy and male potency. Recall what was discussed in *Chapter 4* on the importance of oils in Lingam massage.

Let us move forward in time and move to the East, to the lands of India. Here, Tantra becomes a central philosophy. Ancient Tantric texts, such as the Kama Sutra (Vatsyayana, 400 BC), already detailed techniques and postures to maximize pleasure and spiritual connection. But did you know that these texts didn't just talk about postures? Within their pages are detailed descriptions of massages, caresses and techniques designed to elevate pleasure to a spiritual plane.

Not far away, in China, the Taoists believed that sexual energy, or 'jing', was the vital force that drove life. Texts such as the "Classic of the Yellow Emperor's Internal Medicine" (Huangdi Neijing, 2600 B.C.) stress the importance of conserving and cultivating this energy for health and longevity. Here, Lingam massage was seen not only as a tool for pleasure, but also as a healing technique.

And now, how about moving to the New World? In the lands of Mesoamerica, civilizations such as the Maya and Aztecs saw sexual energy as a powerful force that could connect with the gods. Rituals involving dances, chants and massages were performed to honor the deities and ensure the fertility of the land and its people.

With all this in mind, you can't help but wonder: How is it that, despite vast cultural and geographic differences, we find such similar patterns in the way ancient cultures approached the art of male pleasure? The answer, though complex, leads us to a universal truth: the search for ecstasy, for pleasure, for connection with something greater than oneself, is inherent to being human.

So, as you continue this journey with me, I encourage you to reflect on these traditions, to imagine the hands of ancient practitioners, to feel the energy they have transmitted through the centuries. Because, at the end of the day, we all seek the same thing: a connection, an understanding, an experience that transcends the ordinary and takes us to the very heart of the divine.
Perhaps, as you walk through this ancestral journey, you may wonder, "What about modern practices? How have these ancient rituals been transformed over time?" It's a fascinating

question that leads us to explore how age-old traditions have been adapted, reinvented and enriched by current generations.

Today, many of these ancient practices have found their way into modern therapies. For example, in alternative medicine clinics in Europe and North America, it is common to find therapists integrating Tantric and Taoist techniques into their Lingam massage sessions. These modern fusions combine traditional knowledge with the advances of current science, creating truly unique experiences.

And now, take a moment to visualize this: you are in a luxury spa, where the environment is carefully designed with scents, lights and sounds to create an oasis of tranquility. A therapist, trained in the ancient techniques we've explored, begins the session with a guided meditation. As your mind relaxes, your body begins to respond to the massage, where every touch is an echo of past traditions, but with the focus and precision of modern techniques.

We live in a golden age for personal discovery and sensual exploration. As Sarah Bly points out in her Modern Tantra: A Path to Embodied Spirituality (2017), never before have we had access to so much information and diversity of practices. From workshops in big cities to retreats in exotic destinations, the opportunities to learn and experience are vast.

But it's not just the environment that has evolved. Today, men of all ages, sexual orientations and cultural backgrounds are rediscovering and redefining what male pleasure means. It's a collective awakening, a quiet but powerful revolution. And you, dear reader, are part of this movement.

Of course, we cannot talk about modernity without mentioning the influence of technology. In the digital age, online communities have become vital spaces for sharing experiences, tips and techniques. Apps, videos and tutorials allow anyone, anywhere in the world, to access this vast universe of knowledge.

A shining example of how technology and tantra can merge is the book "Digital Desire: How Technology Shapes Intimacy" (R. Patel, 2019). Patel explores how digital tools can be used to intensify and enhance the tantric experience, merging the ancient with the modern in a seamless dance.

So what does all this mean to you? It means that you are in a unique place and time in history. A crossroads where the old meets the new, where age-old traditions mingle with the innovations of the present. And in the midst of all this, you have the opportunity to design your own path, to decide how you want to explore, experience and express your sensuality.

Perhaps it inspires you to learn more, participate in a workshop, explore an app or simply experiment with your partner. Whatever path you choose, remember that each step you take is an echo of thousands of years of history, and at the same time, an invitation to create your own future. And as you embark on this adventure, always remember: the true essence of Lingam massage and male pleasure is connection. With yourself, with your partner and with the vast and wondrous tapestry of humanity.

Continuing on this fascinating journey through the world of Lingam and its practices, it is important not to forget how each generation leaves its mark, creating a continuum between the past and the present. And just as we have explored ancient rituals and modern practices, it is essential to understand that this evolution is far from having reached its end point.

Think about what the future of Lingam massage will look like. Imagine the techniques that are yet to be discovered, the innovations that will emerge and how these practices will continue to be an endless source of connection and pleasure for generations to come. It's an exciting thought, isn't it?

Experts in the field, such as David Jones in "Tantra of Tomorrow: The Future of Sensual Exploration" (2022), suggest that we are on the cusp of a new era. Jones proposes that Tantric and Lingam massage practices will benefit from emerging technologies and changes in our understanding of the human mind and body. Virtuality, augmented reality, artificial intelligence? How will these influence our experience of pleasure?

And as you immerse yourself in these futuristic possibilities, don't forget the essence of it all: the human desire for connection, for understanding, for touch and ecstasy. As Eleanor Thompson notes in "Touching Eternity: Ancient Rituals in the Modern Age" (2015), no matter how much technology advances or how sophisticated we become as a society, there will always be an intrinsic longing to reach that state of pure joy and connection that practices like Lingam massage can offer.

Now, think about your own journey. Since you began reading this book, you have acquired a wealth of knowledge that goes beyond simple techniques. You've traveled ancient paths, immersed yourself in modern practices, and dreamed of the possibilities of tomorrow. And as each chapter unfolds, you find yourself more empowered, more connected and more in tune with the true art of pleasure.

Do you feel ready to move forward? In the next chapter, we'll navigate the waters of essential precautions and care. Because, as with any journey, it's crucial to ensure that your experience is not only rewarding but also safe. You'll discover how to ensure maximum satisfaction while taking care of yourself and your partner, allowing the experience to be genuinely transformative.

Be tempted by the promise of what follows. The next chapter will not only educate you, but equip you with the tools to make every shared moment a symphony of sensations, balanced with safety and confidence. So take a deep breath, and move forward with determination and curiosity toward the next step of this enlightening journey. I'll be waiting for you there.

Chapter 20: Precautions and Care: Ensuring a Safe Experience

As you delve into the vast world of Lingam massage, did you ever stop to consider the responsibility that comes with having the power to bestow such deep and meaningful pleasure? Now, dear reader, let me ask a question you may not have asked yourself before: are you sure you are guaranteeing a completely safe experience for your partner?

The beauty and power of Lingam massage is undeniable. But, as with any art, caution is essential. Pleasure and safety must walk hand in hand. As Margaret North said in her book "The Sensual Art: Pleasure and Safety in Harmony" (2018), "The art of pleasure is a delicate balance between giving and protecting. One cannot exist without the other." And yes, it's true. When exploring new heights of ecstasy, it is crucial to ensure that the necessary precautions are taken.

The art of Lingam massage, as you have seen in previous chapters, is not just about techniques and practices. It is about a deep connection and intimate understanding between two human beings. And that connection can be affected if safety and care are not prioritized.

Because, although it may seem trivial to some, thinking about safety and well-being is not simply an act of precaution. It is an act of love, of respect for oneself and for the person to whom we are giving this unique experience.

So why is this chapter on precautions and care so vital? Because, dear reader, just as an artist would not let his masterpiece be stained, neither should you allow such a deeply connective and transformative experience to be tarnished by carelessness.

If you recall in Chapter 4, where we discussed tools and oils, I introduced you to the concept of essential preparations for the ritual. And while that chapter provided an excellent foundation, it is crucial to delve deeper into the specific precautions.

Have you ever thought about the allergic reactions that could arise from certain oils? Or the importance of communicating with your partner to make sure you are both on the same page when it comes to boundaries and desires? Precautions and care are not mere "add-ons" to Lingam massage. They are the foundation that ensures that the experience is genuinely revealing and beneficial for both of you.

As you progress through this chapter, you will find not only practical advice and guidance, but also an invitation to reflect on your own practice and to consider how you can make it safer and more rewarding. Because, ultimately, what matters is not only the pleasure you provide, but also the confidence, safety, and care that accompany that pleasure.

So, are you ready to embark on this essential journey? Ready to ensure that every Lingam massage experience you provide is safe, loving and deep? Because I assure you, this knowledge will change your practice and allow you to give and receive pleasure with renewed confidence. And so, dear reader, we begin this journey of caution and care.

When embarking on the world of massage, many forget a fundamental truth: the body is a sacred temple, full of secrets and delicate structures that require our deepest respect and care. Without a doubt, exploring this temple is one of the most sublime experiences one can have. But, like an astute traveler, it is essential that you are armed with the right knowledge to ensure that your exploration is safe and mutually beneficial.

Within the wide range of oils and tools that can be used in Lingam massage, each has its own properties, benefits and possible contraindications. Not all oils are suitable for all skin types, and some tools, if not used correctly, can cause more harm than good.

Jennifer Steinway in her book "The Delicate Art of Touch" (2005) mentions: "Oil is to massage what the brush is to paint". And she is right. A good oil can enhance and transform the massage experience, while the wrong one can trigger allergic reactions or simply not be fit for purpose. For example, sweet almond oil is known for its softening properties and is suitable for most skin types. However, what if your partner is allergic to nuts? This is where knowledge becomes power. Power to choose what is suitable and safe.

What about the tools you can use to enhance your massage? From feathers to hot stones, each tool can take massage to new levels of ecstasy. But it's essential to use them with caution. A stone that is too hot can cause burns, and a tool used with too much force can cause bruising or internal damage. Therefore, like a master craftsman who knows and respects his tools, it is vital that you familiarize yourself with each instrument you use in massage.

Now, have you ever stopped to consider the importance of open and honest communication during massage? It's crucial.

As Michael Hudson wrote in "The Symphony of Intimacy" (2012), "In the game of intimacy, communication is not only the key, it is the instrument, the score and the melody itself." Always ask your partner if they are comfortable, if there is anything they would like you to do differently, or if there is anything they would like to explore. A word, a gesture or even a whisper at the right time can make all the difference.

Therefore, this journey is not only about techniques and tools, but also about how to approach the art of Lingam massage with a deep sense of responsibility and care. It is a dance between two souls, and like any dance, it is essential to know the steps and move with grace and caution.

Let's go deeper into this fascinating and delicate territory of precautions and care, allowing us to see it not only as simple "safety measures", but as essential components to elevate the act of massage to a transcendental art.

Imagine for a moment that you are an explorer, and you find yourself in an unknown land. The wind is blowing gently, the landscape is unfamiliar, and every step you take is a promise of discovery. Now, imagine you hold a map in your hand. This map guides you, avoiding dangers and leading you to hidden treasures. Knowledge of precautions and care is that map in the world of Lingam massage. What would happen if you ventured into this world without that map? You could get lost, or worse, cause harm without realizing it.

Take, for example, the simple action of applying pressure. In his acclaimed book "The Dynamics of Touch" (1998), Lawrence Miller described how pressure can be a double-edged sword. While proper pressure can trigger surges of pleasure, improper pressure can cause pain or, in the worst case, injury. It's essential to learn to "read" your partner, understanding how much pressure is right and when to back off. Now, imagine you are practicing a massage and you apply pressure to a sensitive area. Your partner feels a sharp pain, can you visualize that moment, and do you feel the need to know exactly how to act in that situation?

Here is another aspect that is vital: understanding about communicable diseases and how to avoid their spread. While Lingam massage is not a traditional sexual activity, the closeness and contact with bodily fluids make it an intimate act. As Dr. Elizabeth Hall mentions in "Intimacy & Health" (2010), it is essential to be informed and prepared. Wearing gloves, choosing appropriate oils and hygiene are crucial.

And, speaking of oils, here's a little mental exercise for you. Imagine you're standing in front of a vast collection of aromatic oils. Each bottle emits a unique scent. Now, think about your partner and his or her skin. Which oil would be best: coconut oil, which is moisturizing and has a mild scent? Or perhaps jojoba oil, known for its healing properties? Each choice has implications, and knowing the properties of each oil can make the difference between a good experience and an extraordinary one.

All this leads to one conclusion: knowledge is not only power, but also responsibility. By learning about precautions and care, you are not only ensuring the safety of your partner, but you are also elevating your skill in the art of Lingam massage to unsuspected levels. Because, at the end of the day, true mastery is not just about techniques, but the ability to use those techniques wisely and carefully. And now that you have these tools in your arsenal, are you ready to continue your journey and discover more secrets that await you in the next chapter?

The world of Lingam massage is vast, but like any other discipline, it also has its risks. However, with the right knowledge, these risks can be easily managed and avoided. By diving into the deep waters of caution and care, we find ourselves sailing in a sea full of responsibility and empathy. Because, after all, the goal is to give pleasure, not to cause pain or discomfort.

Recall the words of Alan Watts in "The Way of Zen" (1957), where he said, "True wisdom is found in deep understanding and delicate care." This quote is particularly relevant here. In practicing Lingam massage, we are not only seeking to give pleasure, but also to ensure that that pleasure is given in the safest and most caring way possible.

It's easy to overlook the importance of care when we're in the heat of the moment, immersed in passion and connection. But, as Samuel Harper rightly said in "The Art of Connection" (2001), "Care is the glue that binds passion and security together." And he couldn't be more right. Without care, passion could become dangerous. Without passion, care could become mechanical. It is the balance between these two that we seek.

Now, imagine you are on a road trip. The landscape is constantly changing, offering new sights and experiences. Every curve, every incline, every stretch of road, has its own challenges and rewards. Now, imagine that this journey is your Lingam massage experience. The precautions and care we've discussed are like the signs on the road, guiding you, protecting you, making sure you reach your destination safely.

In summary, this chapter has been an essential reminder of the importance of care and caution in Lingam massage. But don't worry, the journey is not over yet. In fact, we are preparing for a new adventure.

And here's a little surprise for you: the next chapter will take you on an even deeper journey, exploring the connection between Lingam massage and sexual health. How can Lingam massage improve sexual health? What hidden benefits await to be discovered? Well, the answer to these questions and many more await you in Chapter 21. So why wait? Step into this fascinating journey and discover the secrets that await you. The real magic begins now.

Chapter 21: Relationship between Lingam Massage and Sexual Health

If you've ever stopped to think about how to improve your sexual health, you've probably come across numerous solutions. From pills and treatments to diets and therapies. But have you ever considered Lingam massage as a powerful tool to boost your sexual well-being? Probably, if you've immersed yourself in the previous chapters, you're already beginning to see the connection. But if you still have doubts, I invite you to go on this journey with me.

To begin, let me ask you a question that might alter your perspective: Which do you think is more beneficial, treating the symptoms or understanding and addressing the root of the problem? It doesn't take a genius to understand that the second option is the smarter one. And that is precisely what we are about to explore.

Sexual health is more than just the ability to maintain an erection or reach orgasm. It is about understanding, connection and, most importantly, balance. Lingam massage, more than just a pleasure ritual, is a powerful tool that opens the door to this much desired harmony.

While some people may still see it simply as an act of pleasure, what we have learned in previous chapters tells us otherwise. It is a path to self-awareness, exploration, and sexual well-being (Chapter 15: Beyond Orgasm: The Spiritual Dimension of Pleasure). By understanding male anatomy and energy, we not only improve our ability to give and receive pleasure, but also enhance our sexual health.

The renowned sexologist Dr. Alfred Kinsey in "Sexual Behavior in the Human Male" (1948) said: "Sex is one of the nine reasons for reincarnation. The other eight are irrelevant." Wow, that's a bold statement, isn't it? But behind the humor, Kinsey was highlighting the intrinsic importance of a healthy sex life to the human experience.

As we begin this exploration of the relationship between Lingam massage and sexual health, I invite you to pause and reflect. How much do you value your sexual well-being? How much time and energy do you invest in it?

We often worry about our physical health, our mental health, our diet, but what about our sexual health? Although it is a vital part of our being, it is often neglected or forgotten. Lingam massage offers us a unique opportunity to rediscover and revalue this essential dimension of our existence.

This chapter is an invitation to discover the richness of Lingam massage and its potential to transform not only your sex life, but your overall health. I do not promise you an easy path. But, as the proverb says, "the journey of a thousand miles begins with a single step." And I guarantee that every step along the way will be worth it.

Before we continue, I would like you to do something. Imagine you are in a garden full of flowers and plants. Each plant represents a part of your being. What does the plant that symbolizes your sexual health look like? Is it blooming or wilting? Now imagine giving it water, light and love. Imagine how it changes and blossoms. That is the transformation that Lingam massage can offer.

With that image in mind, I invite you to go ahead and dive into the depths of the relationship between Lingam massage and sexual health. Because, at the end of the day, it's not just about pleasure, it's about total wellness.

Delving deeper into the relationship between Lingam massage and sexual health uncovers a universe of connections and benefits beyond our initial expectations. Sexual health is multifaceted and, like any other aspect of our health, requires attention, understanding and care. Now, let the words of experts in the field of human sexuality guide us through this intricate labyrinth.

John Money, in his work "Love and Love Sickness" (1980), writes about the importance of a healthy sex life and its direct connection to a person's emotional and psychological well-being. Lack of understanding and communication in the sexual realm can lead to a variety of complications. From relationship problems to mental health issues, everything can be interconnected.

In this light, Lingam massage stands as a bridge of communication, a tool for self-exploration and, ultimately, a form of therapy. It allows you to communicate with yourself and your partner on levels that transcend words. It is a dance of energies and sensations that connects you deeply with your desires, your fears and your longings.

Now, ask yourself: how much do you really know about your body and its reactions? How many times have you ignored signals your body has given you, relegating its messages to oblivion? The wisdom of the body is profound and, as we mentioned in Chapter 3, discovering the masculine universe is a journey worth undertaking. Because by doing so, you not only enrich your sex life, but also improve your overall health and well-being.

Consider what Shere Hite says in "The Hite Report" (1976), "Our approach to sexuality is deeply rooted in the idea of performance, rather than pleasure and connection." While Hite was referring specifically to female sexuality, her message is universal. We have moved away from authentic pleasure and focused too much on meeting expectations and standards.

Lingam massage is therefore a return to the authentic. It is a pause in the frenzy of everyday life, a space where time seems to stand still and where you give yourself permission to feel, to explore and to be. There are no judgments, no expectations. Just you and the infinitude of the present moment.

It's fascinating how something as simple as a massage can trigger such a depth of understanding and connection. But as with everything in life, the simplest things are often the most powerful.

So, as we continue this journey, I want you to reflect: are you ready to let go of your preconceptions and embark on this adventure? Are you ready to discover all that Lingam massage has to offer? Because, I assure you, this is just the beginning.

Continuing on this fascinating journey, it is vital that we focus on specific examples that illustrate the importance and power of Lingam massage in relation to sexual health. Sometimes words and theories can be abstract, but concrete examples anchor us to reality and allow us to visualize and practice in our minds.

Imagine, for a moment, Daniel, a 35-year-old man who has spent much of his adult life feeling a disconnect with his body. Social pressures and self-imposed expectations have led him to a sex life that, while active, lacks true meaning and connection. Sound familiar? It's possible that many men can relate to him.

Now, Daniel stumbles upon the world of Lingam massage. At first skeptical, he decides to give it a try. What he experiences during that session is revealing. He feels areas of his body that he has never felt before. He realizes that there are areas, as we mentioned in Chapter 10, that are "forgotten zones," points that, when stimulated correctly, can lead to unimaginable heights of pleasure.

This, in itself, is a revelation. But it goes further. In subsequent sessions, Daniel begins to release repressed emotions. During one session, tears flow, not of pain, but of release. He realizes that massage is not only teaching him about his body but also about his mind and soul.

As Virginia E. Johnson highlights in her co-written "Human Sexual Response" (1966) with William Masters, the human body and its sexual response are intricate and connected to our psyche. What we feel physically has emotional repercussions and vice versa.

So what changed in Daniel after his Lingam massage sessions? He became more self-aware, more present in his interactions, not only sexually but also in his daily life. He began to understand that pleasure is not a selfish act, but a path to self-discovery. Instead of constantly seeking external gratification, he began to explore the richness of his inner world.

Do you identify with parts of Daniel's story? Or maybe you know someone who has gone through something similar? The truth is, his story is not unique. It mirrors many men who have discovered the magic of Lingam massage and how it can transform not only their sexual health but their life in general.

And if you still doubt its impact, I invite you to read on. Because there is more to discover, more to learn, and more to experience. Because Lingam massage is not just a technique; it is a journey to the very core of your being.

As we delve into the rich tapestry of Lingam massage and its profound link to sexual health, we cannot fail to mention the work of important figures in the field of human sexuality.

Alfred Kinsey, in his seminal "Kinsey Report" (1948), discovered that male sexuality was far more complex than previously thought. Like Lingam Massage, Kinsey argued that the understanding of male sexuality went beyond simple action and reaction. It was an intricate dance of emotions, sensations and connections.

But why is this connection between Lingam massage and sexual health so crucial? Well, just like a car needs regular maintenance to function properly, the human body, and more specifically sexual health, requires attention and care. By incorporating Lingam massage into your life, you are not only increasing pleasure, but also promoting optimal sexual health. As you explore and connect with your body in new and exciting ways, you open the door to a world of self-discovery.

Just as every story has its chapters, every chapter has its highlights. We have explored the vital relationship between Lingam massage and sexual health. We have understood how this ancient art can be a powerful tool to enhance not only pleasure, but also overall sexual health. But the journey does not end here.

As you look ahead, what if I told you that your diet and habits can influence your Lingam massage experience? Yes, what you eat, how you move, and your daily routines can enhance or detract from your sexual experience.

I invite you to continue with me in the next chapter, where we'll unlock the secrets of how diet and healthy habits can improve your Lingam massage experience and, by extension, your sex life as a whole. If you're ready to take your experience to the next level, to discover how your daily choices can influence your most intimate moments, wait no longer. The following page promises revelations that will change your perspective and, who knows, maybe even transform your life.

Chapter 22: The Influence of Food and Healthy Habits

You've heard the saying, right? "You are what you eat." It's a phrase you've probably heard ad nauseam, but have you ever considered how your diet and daily habits affect your sex life? We're not just talking about how you feel about yourself or your energy level, but how your body responds, gets aroused and connects during an intimate encounter. Food is not just fuel; it's information for the body, and what you choose to eat and how you choose to live your life can have a profound impact on your most intimate experiences.

Imagine for a moment that your body is a precious instrument, delicate yet strong, capable of producing the most beautiful melodies. Wouldn't you want to tune it properly, give it the best possible care and attention? Or would you treat it carelessly, leave it out of tune, and still expect it to produce heavenly music? That's how you should view your body and your sexual health: as an instrument that deserves the best attention, don't you think?

Your sexuality and the pleasure you experience are not isolated from the rest of your life. Just as Lingam massage, mentioned in previous chapters, requires conscious attention to atmosphere, breathing and technique, it also requires attention to your overall health and lifestyle habits.

Let's take a concrete example. According to Dr. Dean Ornish in his book "Dr. Dean Ornish's Program for Reversing Heart Disease" (1990), a diet high in saturated fats and processed foods can lead to atherosclerosis, which is the hardening of the arteries. This, in turn, can reduce blood flow to the penis, which can affect a man's ability to have an erection. So yes, that burger with extra cheese might not be your best ally in the bedroom!

On the other hand, nitric oxide-rich foods such as beets, spinach and nuts can improve circulation and potentially increase sensation and pleasure. And it's not just food; regular exercise, meditation and stress management also play a key role. Research suggests that yoga, mentioned in Patanjali's "Yoga Sutras" (about 400 B.C.), not only improves flexibility and reduces stress, but may also improve libido and sexual function.

The connection between what you eat, how you take care of yourself and your sex life is nothing new, but it's something we often forget or ignore in our busy lives. What if I told you that by making small adjustments to your diet and daily routine you could drastically improve your sex life? Would you be willing to make those changes?

Think about it. When you fuel your body with the best, you not only look and feel better, but you also set yourself up for richer, deeper experiences in all aspects of your life, including sex. So the next time you're faced with a food choice, think about what you really want: a moment of fleeting pleasure on the palate or a whole night of passion and deep connection?

While these tips and insights are just the tip of the iceberg, I invite you to continue exploring with me in the following sections how other habits and choices can influence your Lingam massage experience and ultimately your overall sex life. After all, wisdom and self-discovery is a journey, and each step you take brings you closer to ecstasy. Are you ready to discover more?

Now, when we talk about healthy habits, what comes to mind first? Maybe you think of specific diets, exercise or morning routines. And yes, those are all crucial components, but there's so much more at play. Healthy habits are not just actions; they are a state of mind, an attitude, a way of looking at and living life.

Dr. Helen Fisher, in her acclaimed book "Anatomy of Love" (1992), explores how chemicals in our brain, such as dopamine, influence attraction and desire. And guess what? These chemicals can be influenced by what you eat and how you live. So you're not just nourishing your body, you're nourishing your feelings and emotions.

So what can we do to nourish not only our bodies but also our souls and deepest desires? Here are some tips backed by science and expert wisdom:

1. **Consumption of antioxidants**: Fruits such as blueberries, strawberries and pomegranates are rich in antioxidants, which protect the body against free radicals. A healthy body at the cellular level is more receptive to pleasure. Michael Greger, in his How Not To Die (2015), talks in depth about how a plant-based diet can transform your health and well-being.
2. **Stay hydrated**: Water is essential for circulation and overall health. And, as we have explored in previous chapters, circulation plays a crucial role in sensation and pleasure.
3. **Practice meditation**: Stress is a desire killer. Meditation and mindfulness techniques can help you

be present during your intimate experiences, enhancing connection and pleasure. Jon Kabat-Zinn, in his book "Living Fully in Crisis" (1994), offers practical techniques for incorporating mindfulness into your daily life.

4. **Laugh more**: Did you know that laughing can improve your sexual health and well-being? Laughter releases endorphins, reduces stress and improves circulation. So, the next time you're tempted to take life too seriously, remember that a good laugh may be just what you need to ignite the spark.

Imagine that your body is a garden. Everything you put into it, from your food to your thoughts and emotions, affects how it grows and flourishes. And at the center of that garden is your sex life, waiting to be nurtured and cared for. Just as a flower needs water, sunshine and care to bloom, your sex life needs a balanced diet, exercise, meditation and laughter to thrive.

Now, I want you to ask yourself a question: What steps are you willing to take to nurture your inner garden? Are you ready to make your sex life and well-being a priority? Because, at the end of the day, it's not just about sex or pleasure; it's about living a full and rich life in every way. It's time to commit to that journey.

So you've decided to commit to that journey. A wise choice. But what happens when you make the conscious decision to nourish both your body and your mind? Well, my dear reader, the magic starts to happen.

Let's talk about some practical examples to illustrate how food and healthy habits can directly influence your sexual experience. You may have heard of aphrodisiac food, but did you know that its effect goes beyond the mythological?

Chocolate: According to research published in "The Science of Aphrodisiacs" (Lyttle, 1993), chocolate contains phenylethylamine, a substance that releases endorphins and can improve mood. So why not incorporate a little chocolate into your foreplay? Next time you're with your partner, try a massage using cocoa oil, or perhaps a few small pieces of chocolate that you can enjoy together.

Avocado: This fruit has been valued for its aphrodisiac properties for centuries. It contains vitamin E, which helps maintain energy and fight free radicals that can damage tissues and organs. Did you know that the Aztecs considered the avocado tree so powerful that virgins could not go out alone during the harvest season?

Ginger: This root has been used in traditional Chinese medicine for thousands of years to increase circulation and improve energy. Imagine incorporating a little ginger into your meals to ignite that inner spark. Plus, as Dr. Andrew Weil mentions in his book "Eating Well for Optimum Health" (2000), ginger has anti-inflammatory properties that can help keep the body in its best shape.

But beyond food, let's remember that healthy habits also play a crucial role. In this sense, exercise not only improves circulation and endurance, but also boosts self-confidence. Have you ever noticed that euphoric feeling after a good workout? That's your blood circulating, your body releasing endorphins. And yes, this can translate into increased energy and sex drive.

Let's think about it for a moment. You've heard the phrase, "You are what you eat." But, I challenge you to look at it from a different perspective: "You are what you consume." From the food you choose, to the programs you watch, to the books you read, to the thoughts you allow into your mind. All of these feed your being.

So, here's a question to ponder: What are you choosing to consume today? And I don't just mean your food, but everything that allows you to nourish and enrich your experience on this earth. Are you choosing elements that uplift you, or are you indulging in habits that ultimately drain you?

Getting into the heart of the matter, one cannot help but marvel at the complexity of our biology and how everything is interconnected. The idea that something as everyday as the food you eat or the daily habits you adopt can have such a profound effect on your sex life and well-being is simply astounding. It is that complexity that drives us to explore more and more and to marvel at how, in the act of taking care of ourselves, we are also nurturing our sex lives.

Now, as we get into this deeper topic, it is critical that you let yourself be guided by those experts who have devoted years of research and study. One name that deserves special attention is Dr. Michael Greger, author of "How Not To Die" (2015). Greger points out the vital importance of a plant-based diet not only for longevity but also for sexual health. Through a comprehensive analysis of multiple studies, he reveals how diet can influence cardiovascular health and thus erectile function.

But it's not just erectile function that's at stake. Libido, energy, mental clarity, all of these elements that contribute to a full and rewarding sexual experience, are influenced by what you eat and how you live. The idea here is not to overwhelm you with information but to inspire you to make informed choices, choices that benefit you in the present and set you up for a healthy, active future.

Taking a moment to reflect, you may be asking yourself, what does all this mean to me? Well, it means you have the power. The power to make decisions that not only improve your overall health, but also elevate your sexual experience. And who wouldn't want that?

Now, as we prepare to close this chapter, I invite you to move forward. To continue on this journey of self-discovery, because, after all, isn't that what life really is? A journey, a constant exploration.

As we open the next chapter, we will immerse ourselves in the voices of those who have walked this path before you. Real testimonies, shared experiences. Each story is unique, but they all have one thing in common: the search for deeper connection, for more intense pleasure. Prepare to be inspired, moved, and perhaps even to see a reflection of yourself in their words. Because, after all, we are connected on this journey. See you in Chapter 23.

Chapter 23: True Stories: Testimonials and Shared Experiences

Have you ever been curious to witness someone else's intimate experience? Not to invade their privacy, but to learn, to understand better. In the vast arena of male pleasure, many feel alone in their journey, wondering, "Am I the only one who feels this?" But the answer is a resounding no. And here, in Chapter 23, you'll dive into true stories, vibrant testimonials and shared experiences that will shed light on several men's journey through Lingam massage and what they discovered in the process.

Imagine a world in which we could openly share our most intimate experiences, not for the purpose of bragging or causing envy, but for the purpose of learning and growing. In that world, your curiosity would be satiated, your questions answered and your insecurities dispelled. I invite you to enter that world here and now.

Why is it so crucial to read about real experiences? Because they are the compass that guides us, the confirmation that we are not alone, and sometimes the inspiration we need to take the next step in our own journey. Stories have the power to connect, to humanize, to teach. As you read the experiences of others, I invite you to reflect on your own experiences, what can you learn from them, how do they compare to what you are about to discover?

Bernard Shaw, in his play "Man and Superman" (1903), said, "If you have an apple and I have an apple and we exchange them, then you and I will still have an apple each. But if you have an idea and I have an idea and we exchange them, then we will both have two ideas." It is in this spirit of sharing and multiplying knowledge that we present these stories.

Have you ever stopped to think how much you could learn from others if you dare to listen? Experiences, no matter how intimate, can be the doorway to a world of understanding and learning. So relax, keep an open mind and prepare to be transported through the words and experiences of others, as you step into a journey that promises to be revealing. For, after all, stories are the fabric from which humanity is woven. As you delve deeper into this sea of experiences, it is inevitable to remember the words of the famous writer Oscar Wilde in "The Picture of Dorian Gray" (1890), "Experiencing is the only form of knowledge". The testimonials we will explore are not mere words on a page; they are lives lived, emotions felt and lessons learned.

Think about it for a moment, how many times have you had a life-changing experience and wanted to share it with the world? Now, imagine if every man who has experienced Lingam massage could share his journey with you. Wouldn't that be a rich tapestry of knowledge and understanding? You are about to immerse yourself in such stories.

Tomas, a 35 year old engineer, shared with us his first encounter with Lingam massage. He had read about the benefits and decided to try it as a gift to himself. His first time, he described, was "a roller coaster of emotions." At first, the vulnerability overwhelmed him, but as he surrendered to the process, he found a deep connection to his own self. What began as a simple quest for physical pleasure, transformed into a journey of self-discovery and spirituality. At the end of his session, Tomas shed tears, not of sadness, but of gratitude and revelation.

These types of testimonials echo what many men have experienced but don't always feel comfortable sharing. Society often labels male vulnerability as a weakness, but isn't it more of a strength to admit, explore and embrace all facets of oneself?

Now, if Tomas' experience makes you think that Lingam massage is only for the spiritual or introspective, think again. Another testimonial, from Enrique, a 42-year-old lawyer, shares a more earthy approach. For him, the massage was "a break from his busy life, an oasis of pleasure in a desert of stress." Enrique wasn't looking for a spiritual awakening, he just wanted to relax and enjoy a moment to himself. And that is precisely what he got. Recalling Henry Miller's words in "Sexus" (1949), "The aim of the body is to discover how much pleasure it can endure without breaking down." Enrique found that frontier and crossed it with enthusiasm, emerging renewed.

These stories, and many others we'll introduce you to, underscore a universal truth: every experience is unique, and every person finds in Lingam massage what they're looking for, whether it's a spiritual connection, an escape from routine or just pure pleasure. And you, what will you find?

As we immerse ourselves in these testimonials, there is something deeply human that resonates, a universal desire for connection, understanding and authenticity. Each story carries with it a piece of the storyteller's soul, and as we read them, we find ourselves reflecting on our own experiences, desires and fears.

Valeria, a tantric therapist with over a decade of experience, shared with us the testimony of David, a businessman who was looking to regain the spark in his relationship. David had lost the connection with his partner, both were stuck in a monotonous routine. The Lingam massage, for him, was a revelation. During the session, he remembered the sensations he had forgotten, the tingling in his back, the sting of anticipation, the intimacy of total surrender. Memories of his youth, moments of passion and adventure surfaced. After the session, David felt rejuvenated, full of energy and determination to reconnect with his partner. Valeria quoted him as saying, "I felt like a teenager again, with all the raw emotions and unbridled passion."

But what makes these experiences so powerful? According to Dr. Ian Kerner in "She Comes First" (2004), "The human body is an instrument of pleasure, and like any instrument, it needs to be tuned, understood and played with skill." Lingam massage sessions allow men to tune into their bodies, rediscover their rhythms and pulsations, and open up to deeper levels of pleasure and connection.

Of course, not all testimonials are success stories. Some men, though fewer in number, have encountered challenges during their experience. Santiago, for example, struggled with his own insecurities and fears during his first session. In his testimony, he shared how he faced ghosts from past experiences and how, with the help of his therapist, he was able to overcome those obstacles. It is a reminder that each journey is personal and sometimes facing our fears and vulnerabilities is part of the process.

These stories not only provide insight into the Lingam massage experience from different perspectives, but also highlight the complexity and richness of male pleasure. They teach us that, beyond the physical act, Lingam massage is a portal to a deeper experience, one that touches the soul, mind and body alike.

Before we continue, have you ever stopped to think about the richness of your own experiences? Are there moments, sensations or emotions that you have forgotten or overlooked? Each of us has a story to tell, and every story is valuable.

The stories we have explored so far open a window into a fascinating and diverse world of experiences and feelings. Each testimony is like a brushstroke on a larger canvas, representing the full range of what it means to be human and to experience pleasure. As we navigate these stories, we find patterns, learn from the experiences of others and, perhaps most importantly, see ourselves reflected in their words.

A study by psychologist and author Dr. Albert Richards in his work "The Mirror of Desire" (1998), suggests that the stories others share can act as mirrors, reflecting our own experiences, desires and fears. Through these mirrors, we find validation, understanding and sometimes inspiration to embark on our own journey of self-discovery.

What if I told you that every testimony, every story, is not just a glimpse into the past, but a key to the future? A tool you can use to unlock deeper levels of connection, pleasure and understanding.

The beauty of Lingam massage lies not only in the technique or the anatomy, but in the ability of the practice to take us to unexpected places. Places of vulnerability, strength, passion and peace. Each session is a journey, and each journey is unique.

How can I use what I have learned in this chapter in my daily life? How can I begin my own journey of self-discovery and pleasure? Let me tell you that the path is right in front of you, waiting to be explored.

As we come to the end of this chapter, we are about to embark on an even deeper journey. In the next chapter, "Increasing the Intensity: Advanced Levels of Lingam Massage," I will take you by the hand through advanced techniques and secrets that will allow you to elevate the Lingam massage experience to new heights. I guarantee it will be an unforgettable journey, full of revelations and discoveries. Are you ready to dive deeper into the ocean of pleasure and connection? I look forward to seeing you in the next chapter. The adventure continues.

Chapter 24: Increasing Intensity: Advanced Levels of Lingam Massage

Pleasure, that elusive sensation we all seek, has an almost elusive nature. But imagine for a moment that you have in your hands the power to not only understand it, but to intensify it, elevate it, and unlock dimensions of ecstasy you didn't even know existed. What would you do with that power?

You've reached the point in your journey where the basic understanding of Lingam massage is no longer enough. You've glimpsed the vastness of male pleasure, but are you ready to dive into its depths? Because that's exactly what we're going to do in this chapter. So take a deep breath, because we're about to embark on a journey into advanced levels of this ancient art.

Why is it important to know and understand these advanced levels? Well, as George B. Shaw said in "Man and the Superman" (1903), "Those who look at the world on its surface, lose its essence". Lingam massage is no exception. Like any practice, there are levels of mastery, and each level brings with it deeper benefits and experiences.

You must be asking yourself, "Haven't we already explored everything about Lingam massage?". Although we have touched on its history, its basic techniques and its impact, there is still so much more to discover. Think of it as if you were listening to a symphony. In our first approach, we've enjoyed the main melody, but now, it's time to dive into the intricacies and nuances hidden in the secondary notes, those that you don't notice at first listen, but once you identify them, they change your entire perception of the piece.

Now, how do you increase the intensity and get into these advanced levels of Lingam massage? Remember in **Chapter 6** when we talked about "Breath and Energy"? That's your starting point. Just like a musician needs to tune his instrument to sound perfectly, we also need to prepare ourselves mentally and physically for this intensification.

I want you to reflect for a moment. Think about the last time you experienced pleasure. Was it fleeting? Did you wish it lasted longer? This is where advanced levels can be your ally. By mastering these techniques, you will not only be able to prolong pleasure, but you will also be able to guide it, shape it, and experiment with it in ways you never imagined.

Humorist and writer Mark Twain once remarked, "The difference between the right word and the almost right word is the same as between the lightning bolt and the firefly." So, are you ready to stop chasing fireflies and start directing lightning? Because that's what we're going to do next.

Before continuing, it is important to keep in mind that this path requires patience, practice and, above all, an open mind. So, if you are willing to explore, learn and grow, I invite you to go ahead. Because, at the end of the day, as Lao Tse said in the "Tao Te Ching" (6th century B.C.), "The journey of a thousand miles begins with the first step."

So, dear reader, are you ready to take that step and dive into the advanced levels of Lingam massage? If so, get ready, because the journey ahead is exciting, eye-opening and, without a doubt, transformative.

The journey to mastery in any discipline is always punctuated by unexpected discoveries, nuances that, at first glance, might go unnoticed but which, in reality, become the very essence of the practice. As we move into the higher levels of Lingam massage, one might ask, "What else is there to discover?" Ah, but therein lies the true beauty. It is precisely in those hidden corners that we find the most precious treasures.

We mentioned earlier how breathing is the starting point. But did you know that there are ways to manipulate it to amplify pleasure? In her book "The Power of Breath" (1989), Nancy Zi talks about how different cultures use the breath to achieve altered states of consciousness. Now, what happens if we apply this knowledge to Lingam massage? The answer is simple but powerful: transformation.

Think of pleasure as a flame. With the right breath, we can feed that flame, make it bigger, brighter, and control it at our whim. It is like a dancer who, with a slight movement, can change the direction and rhythm of his dance. This is how breathing becomes our main ally in this advanced stage. Through it, we not only intensify pleasure, but also direct and shape it.

Of course, breathing is not the only factor at play. In "The Dimensions of Touch" (1995), Karen Studd and Laura Cox describe how the type of touch, pressure and rhythm can influence our perception of pleasure. In advanced Lingam massage, these elements must be understood and mastered to perfection. The ability to identify and adapt these nuances is what differentiates an experienced practitioner from a novice.

But have you ever stopped to think about the power of anticipation? That delicious waiting, that game of "almost but not yet" that empowers our experience. In literature, Charles Dickens was a master of this. His stories, originally published in installments, kept readers anxious, waiting for the next chapter. We can take a lesson from Dickens and apply it here. Playing with anticipation, with pacing, with waiting, can be an incredibly powerful tool in our hands.

It is essential to remember that as we explore these advanced levels, communication remains key. As we mentioned in **Chapter 12**, "The Emotional Connection," it is crucial to stay in tune with the person receiving the massage, adjusting our techniques according to their responses and needs.

It is tempting to rush and want to master all these advanced techniques quickly. However, as Aristotle said in "Nicomachean Ethics" (c. 350 B.C.), "What we have to learn, we learn by doing". Therefore, practice is essential. It is a journey, an exploration, a constant learning process in which each session, each experience, is an opportunity to grow and improve.

Closing your eyes for a moment, imagine the infinite possibilities that open up before you. You are an artist, and the body is your canvas. With every touch, with every breath, you are creating a masterpiece of pleasure and connection. So keep going, keep exploring, and remember that in this journey to mastery, the journey is as important as the destination.

With each advance we make in our journey towards a deeper understanding of Lingam massage, we encounter multiple nuances and details that enhance our experience. Here, at this advanced stage, is where the real magic begins to happen. But what exactly is it that makes a technique "advanced"? Is it complexity, finesse, or perhaps it is simply intuition gained through experience? Well, you could say it's a mixture of all of it.

Let's delve into an often forgotten but fundamental aspect: the power of sound. I'm not just referring to background music, although that is crucial as we mentioned in **Chapter 5** on "The Importance of Atmosphere". I am referring to the sounds we produce with our voice, those that reflect our inner state. In his work "The Healing Sound" (2001), Jonathan Goldman talks about how sound frequencies can affect our physiology and psychology. Imagine for a moment, intoning a soft sound, a murmur, while practicing massage, creating a vibration that travels throughout the body and amplifies the sensation.

This brings us to a fascinating concept explored by Anne Cawthorn and Joanne Appleyard in their book "Therapeutic Massage Techniques" (2002). They introduce the idea of "energy return". It is a circle of give and take, where the energy of the masseuse and the receiver flow in tune, and any increase in the energy level of one automatically increases that of the other. This is not mere poetry, it is pure physics.

A practical example might be when the massage therapist senses that the receiver is near a peak of pleasure. Instead of speeding up, the masseuse might slow down, build more anticipation, and use sounds, either with the voice or with tools such as Tibetan bells or quartz bowls. The sound vibrates, and those vibrations interact with brain waves, bringing the receiver into a state of deep relaxation and receptivity.

But this goes beyond simple techniques. It is about developing a deeper understanding, an empathy with the receiver. "The Essence of Massage" (1998) by Darien Pritchard, gives us an insight into how each individual is unique and how each massage session should be tailored to reflect that uniqueness. This involves not only adapting techniques, but also energy, rhythm, atmosphere and, of course, sound.

Now, speaking of examples, imagine for a moment being in a quiet room, with dim lights. The recipient's breathing is deep and regular. At the start, the masseuse uses high-quality essential oils, as we discussed in **Chapter 4**, and combines basic techniques with more intricate movements. But instead of following a set pattern, the masseuse moves with intuition, tuning into the receiver's responses. Sensing a shift in energy, the massage therapist intones a soft sound, perhaps a harmonic chant, and feels how the vibrations amplify each touch, each caress.

This is the level of mastery we refer to. It is where science meets art, and where Lingam massage becomes a dance of energies. It is a world of infinite possibilities, waiting to be explored by those willing to embark on this journey.

Our advanced exploration of Lingam massage has led us down meandering paths of self-discovery and deep connection. It is like navigating a river: sometimes calm and gentle, sometimes intense and full of rapids. But always leading us into an ocean of deeper understanding.

The true essence of an advanced massage lies not in complicated techniques or unexpected twists and turns, but in the ability to stay present and connected, listening and feeling with your whole being. Stephen Russell and Tony Ley in "The Tao of Tantra" (2003) put it beautifully, "Tantra is the way of the heart." It is a reminder that no matter how advanced our abilities are, if they are not imbued with love, understanding and respect, they lack their vital essence.

So how do we achieve this balance between technique and heart? The answer is simple, but not necessarily easy: practice, introspection and openness to intuitive guidance. Recall what we mentioned in **Chapter 6** on "Breath and Energy". It is that constant flow of energy, that dance between giving and receiving, that makes the difference between a good massage and an exceptionally transformative one.

To illustrate, let us recall the great masters of martial arts. It is not their physical strength or their techniques that make them stand out, but their ability to be present, to flow with the situation and adapt to what is presented. In the same way, a master masseuse does not stick rigidly to a set of steps, but adapts, flows and creates a unique dance with each session.

And as we navigate these advanced territories, one aspect stands out brilliantly: the power of intention. It is not enough to simply perform a massage; it is essential to infuse it with a clear and loving intention. As Mikao Usui, founder of Reiki, explains in his 1922 teachings, energy follows intention. Thus, by setting a clear intention of healing, love and connection, every touch, every movement becomes a powerful tool for transformation.

This brings us to a natural close to this chapter. We have traveled through the subtle nuances and vibrant depths of advanced Lingam massage. Are you feeling that spark of curiosity, that desire to learn more? Well, dear reader, the journey is far from over.

The next chapter, "The Inner Journey", will invite you to explore the depths of your own being. You will discover how Lingam massage is not just a physical practice, but a path to self-discovery and self-exploration. An invitation to look within, to connect with your true essence and to discover the hidden treasures that lie waiting to be found. Ready to embark on this inner journey? I promise, it will be an adventure you won't want to miss.

Chapter 25: The Inner Journey: The Path to Self-Discovery and Self-Exploration

Sexuality is not only a form of expression, but also a portal to the deepest part of our being. Have you ever wondered why the most intimate act can arouse such deep emotions, both pleasure and pain? The answer lies in the link between our essence and our sexuality. And this chapter, dear reader, is an invitation to this inner journey, towards self-discovery and self-exploration.

Now, you might be thinking, "I've come all this way looking for advanced Lingam massage techniques and now you're telling me about inner travel and self-exploration. Why should I care?". A valid question, and the answer is simple: because pleasure is not just physical. It is a multidimensional experience that encompasses the mental, the emotional and, yes, the spiritual.

Ask yourself this: Why do you seek to give or receive a Lingam massage? Is it just for the physical pleasure? Or is there something deeper, a longing for connection, to understand and be understood, to touch and be touched not only in the body but also in the soul?

We have mentioned it before, in **Chapter 6: Breath and Energy**. Breathing is the gateway to that inner journey. It is the link between the outer world and the inner world. Through it, we can access altered states of consciousness, where barriers dissolve and we can truly see ourselves and each other.

Philosopher Alan Watts, in his work "The Book of Tao" (1975), talks about how Taoism sees sexuality as a way to reach enlightenment. It is not about repressing or glorifying, but about understanding and flowing. Because, in essence, we are sexual and spiritual beings at the same time.

So, as you dive into the deep waters of this chapter, I invite you to do so with an open mind. Open your heart to the possibilities, to the idea that your sexuality is a bridge to your essence. Think of it as a meditation, where every touch, every sigh, every surge of pleasure is a note in the symphony of your being.

Do you dare to embark on this journey? Don't worry, you won't be alone. Throughout this chapter, I will guide you step by step, sharing with you tools, techniques and, most importantly, the right mindset to embark on this adventure. So, take a deep breath, relax and get ready for a journey like no other.

A journey of self-discovery and self-exploration is not a straight path, but rather a series of curves, ups and downs, setbacks and breakthroughs. As we move forward on this journey, we may discover aspects of ourselves that we had never considered before, or that we had chosen to ignore. It is a process that can be both challenging and revealing. But why is it essential to embark on it? And what does all this have to do with Lingam massage?

When we are children, we are more connected to our authentic selves. However, over time, society, expectations and experiences can cause us to disconnect from that essence. And therein lies the importance of self-discovery:

reconnecting with that essence, remembering who we really are and freeing ourselves from the chains that bind us.

Carl Jung, the eminent Swiss psychologist, in his work "Archetypes and the Tarot" (1959), postulated that we all have a "shadow", a part of us that we reject or deny. And it is only through the confrontation and integration of this shadow that we can achieve true self-acceptance. Imagine Lingam massage as a tool to unblock these shadows, to bring those repressed emotions and desires to the surface, and to give us the opportunity to face and ultimately embrace them.

You may be thinking, "This sounds profound, but how do I do it?". This is where self-exploration comes in. If self-discovery is the what, self-exploration is the how. It is the active process of digging inside ourselves, asking the hard questions and searching for the answers. And yes, Lingam massage can be one of the tools you use on this journey.

Think of Lingam massage not only as a technique to give pleasure, but as a form of meditation. A practice that allows you to tune into your body, your emotions and your energy. Every touch is an invitation to explore, every sensation is a clue to what is hidden in the depths of your being.

Now, are you ready to go deeper into this journey? Exploration is not always easy, but I promise you it will be enriching. And in the process, you'll not only discover more about yourself, but you'll also strengthen your connection with your partner, creating a deeper and more meaningful bond. All you need is an open mind, a willing heart and the right techniques. And if you ever feel lost, remember what we mentioned in **Chapter 12: Emotional Connection**; there is power in vulnerability and in sharing your discoveries with someone you trust.

So, once you've opened the door to self-discovery and self-exploration through Lingam massage, what awaits you when you walk through it? As you dive deeper into this world of sensation and self-knowledge, you will discover that each experience is unique and revealing. But to better visualize it, let's allow a few examples to light the way.

Imagine Alejandro, a man in his thirties. He has always been reserved about his sexuality, due in large part to a strict and conservative upbringing. But, after reading **Chapter 7: The Power of Conscious Touch**, he decided to try Lingam massage. At first, her mind resisted, bound by years of conditioning. However, with time and practice, the barriers began to dissolve. What she discovered was an endless source of pleasure and, more importantly, a path to self-forgiveness and acceptance. Releasing old tensions and blockages, Alejandro found himself in a way he never imagined possible.

Or consider Valeria and Raul, a couple who have been together for more than a decade. Although their love runs deep, routine and daily demands had taken a toll on their intimate connection. However, after introducing Lingam massage into their relationship, as suggested in **Chapter 13: The Role of the Receiver**, they discovered aspects of each other that they had never seen before. Raul, in surrendering to Valeria's caresses, experienced vulnerability, a feeling he had avoided for years. Valeria, for her part, found a deeper sense of empowerment and connection with her partner.

Together, through this practice, they renewed their mutual commitment and passion.

In his book "Sexuality and Spirituality: The Sacred Dance" (1984), Anand Margot talks about how sexuality can be a bridge to spirituality. Through practices such as Lingam massage, we can transcend our physical limitations and connect with something greater than ourselves. Every touch, every breath, every whisper is a prayer, an offering to the divine being that resides in each of us.

So, what discoveries await you on this journey? What secrets are waiting to be unveiled in the depths of your being? There is only one way to find out: by immersing yourself in the experience, surrendering to the moment and allowing Lingam Massage to guide you to your inner truth.

These examples only scratch the surface of what is possible. But what if I told you there is even more? In the depths of this ancient art, there are treasures waiting to be discovered. Are you willing to search for them? Because if you are, the next chapter promises revelations that will change your perspective forever. And as an avid navigator of knowledge and sensations, I invite you to continue sailing towards these unknown and deep waters. Because the real journey, dear reader, has just begun.

As you find yourself on this introspective journey, it is essential to remember that each step, each moment of self-discovery, is a jewel in itself. The facets of these jewels reflect the innumerable truths that reside within you. Each of us carries an ocean of sensations, memories and desires, and

Lingam massage is a compass to help us navigate these turbulent waters.

While we have discussed the technique and theory behind this ancient practice, the real crux of Lingam massage lies in its ability to connect with oneself and others on levels we often overlook. By embracing this art, you offer yourself a priceless gift: the gift of self-understanding.

Now, dear reader, do you remember **Chapter 6: Breath and Energy**? Take a deep breath as you process all you have learned. Let me quote the celebrated author Amelia Hart, in her work "The Awakening of Touch" (1999), who wisely said, "Touch is the non-verbal language of the soul, and through it, we communicate our deepest truths." By exploring Lingam massage, you not only learn techniques and movements, but you also learn the language of the soul, a language that we all speak but few really understand.

We have journeyed together through pages filled with passion, knowledge and discovery. Each chapter has taken you closer to the very essence of what it means to give and receive pleasure, to connect with yourself and your partner on levels never before explored. It has been a journey of learning, liberation and deep self-love.

As I come to the end of this chapter, and of the book itself, I feel a bittersweet feeling. It has been an honor and a privilege to be your guide on this journey, and it saddens me to think that our time together in these pages has come to an end. But, at the same time, it fills me with joy to think of all that awaits you as you put into practice what you have learned.

I want to thank you, from the deepest part of my being, for allowing me to be part of your journey of self-discovery. It has been a real pleasure to share these moments with you. And as this book reaches its conclusion, your journey, dear reader, is just beginning.

I wish you to find pleasure, joy and connection in every corner of your life. May each experience take you to greater heights and depths. May you continue to explore, learn and love with your whole being. And always remember that, in the art of pleasure and connection, the journey is as important as the destination.

With all my love and gratitude, I wish you the best in every step you take. May the paths of life lead you to fulfillment and ecstasy in all its forms. Farewell.

Farewell: Invitation to a timeless journey of pleasure and connection

Just as every great journey begins with a single step, so too comes the moment when the starting point to new adventures presents itself. Throughout this journey, we have traveled a path of knowledge, discovery and deep connection, not only with the ancient art of Lingam massage, but also with the very essence of male pleasure.

Recapping on this adventure, we explored everything from the basics of Tantra, to the rich male anatomy, to the deepest secrets of emotional connection. I introduced you to the importance of creating the right environment, how breathing is the key to deeper connection and how, through the power of conscious touch, you can discover the vastness of the male universe.

We journeyed together through techniques, from the most basic to the most advanced, exploring often forgotten points of arousal and immersing ourselves in waves of excitement. We shared real stories and testimonials, and learned about the precautions necessary to ensure a safe and transformative experience.

Of course, health and wellness are fundamental pillars in this journey, and that is why we delve into the relationship between nutrition, healthy habits and sexual health. The importance of taking care not only of the body, but also of the mind and spirit, has been a constant in this work.

Now that we've come to the end of this tour, you may be wondering, **what's the next step?**

The answer is simple: practice. This reading has provided the tools and knowledge, but it is you who must embark on the practical journey, exploring, discovering and deepening the art of Lingam massage and connection with self and others.

I encourage you to continue your training, perhaps looking for courses or workshops specialized in Lingam or Tantra massage. Stay curious and open to new experiences, and always, always listen to your body and your intuition.

Dear reader, it has been an immense pleasure to share this journey with you. I deeply appreciate your trust and your dedication in every page of this adventure. Remember that the path of self-knowledge and pleasure is eternal, and although this work has come to an end, your journey has just begun.

I wish that the journey fills you with joy, fulfillment and deep connections, both with yourself and those around you.

With all my love and gratitude, I hope you continue to explore, love and discover the mysteries of the male universe.

May you always find pleasure, connection and love on your path.

With love,

Carolina Garcia.

BONUS

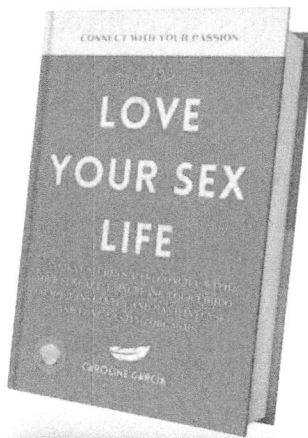

Dear reader, in appreciation of your courage to delve into the corners of your sexuality, I want to offer you this exclusive gift that complements the main book you have just purchased. With this guide you will be able to enjoy your sexual life to the fullest, even if you were never able to or your environment prevented you from doing so. Once you finish reading, you will feel that you are in tune with your sexual essence and your inner being will enjoy joy.

Click Here To Download Your Free Guide >>

https://bit.ly/SEXUALITYUS

Last words

Dear reader,

We come to the end of this exciting journey together. I hope you enjoyed each page as much as I enjoyed writing them for you. If you wish to continue exploring worlds full of emotions, intrigue and passion, I invite you to visit my author page on Amazon.

There you will find a collection of similar works that will take you on new adventures and allow you to immerse yourself in stories that will captivate you once again.

Thank you for being part of this literary journey. I hope our paths cross again between the pages of my books.

With gratitude,

Caroline Garcia

Made in the USA
Las Vegas, NV
19 April 2024